Janner's
Complete Letterwriter

GREVILLE JANNER

Janner's
Complete Letterwriter

THIRD EDITION

Cartoons by Tobi

BUSINESS BOOKS

London   Melbourne   Sydney   Auckland   Johannesburg

Business Books Ltd

An imprint of the Hutchinson Publishing Group

17-21 Conway Street, London W1P 6JD

Hutchinson Publishing Group (Australia) Pty Ltd
PO Box 496, 16-22 Church Street,
Hawthorn, Melbourne, Victoria 3122

Hutchinson Group (NZ) Ltd
32-34 View Road, PO Box 40-086, Glenfield, Auckland 10

Hutchinson Group (SA) (Pty) Ltd
PO Box 337, Bergvlei 2012, South Africa

First published under the title *The Businessman's
Guide to Letter-writing and to the Law on Letters,* 1970
Reprinted 1972, 1974
Second edition 1977
Reprinted 1979, 1981 (twice)
Reprinted 1982
Third edition (with new title) 1983
Reprinted 1984 (twice)

Set in Times

Printed and bound in Great Britain by
Anchor Brendon Ltd, Tiptree, Essex

British Library Cataloguing in Publication Data
Janner, Greville
   Janner's complete letterwriter
   1. Letter-writing
   I. Title
   806.6   PE1483

ISBN 0 09 151800 8 (cased)
     0 09 151801 6 (paperback)

In loving memory of
Emeritus Chief Rabbi Sir Israel Brodie, KBE
and for
Lady Brodie
who taught me that 'respect goes before the law'
– with great affection –

Contents

Introduction   *xi*

Part 1   FORM AND FORMALITIES

Chapter 1   The Shape of a Letter   3
           2   Hail and Farewell – for the Start and Finish
               of a Letter   4
           3   Signatures and Postscripts   6
           4   Lists and Schedules   8
           5   References – on Letters   9
           6   The Layout of a Letter   10
           7   Acknowledgements – and Standard Forms   12
           8   Names and Titles   15

Part Two   STYLE AND GRAMMAR

Chapter 9   Style   23
          10   Grammatical Thoughts, Ungrammatical Words
               – and Adult Remedies   24
          11   Punctuation, Self-expression – and the Limits
               to Formal Grammar   26
          12   Brevity   28
          13   The Choice of Words – and Words to the Wise   29
          14   Clarity   31
          15   Clichés   33
          16   Officialese   35
          17   Wit and Humour   36
          18   Similes and Metaphors – Mixed and Other   41

Part 3   TACT AND TACTICS

Chapter 19   Modesty Matters   47
          20   Flattery – and the Great You Are   49
          21   Praise Him . . .   55
          22   The Art of Rudeness   56
          23   Rude Retorts – at Leisure   60

24   Tearing off Strips – Plus Warnings and
     Complaints   63
25   The Other Cheek   65
26   In a Tight Corner   65
27   Apologies   69
28   Lies – Black and White   70
29   Replies to Lies   73
30   On a Personal Note   75
31   Letters Overseas – Customers and their
     Customs   76
32   The Human Races   79
33   Follow-up   80
34   Introductions and References   81

Part 4   LETTERS FOR OCCASIONS

Chapter 35   Letters that Sell   87
           36   Applying for Posts – and Selling Yourself   89
           37   Interviews for Jobs   94
           38   Retirement and Thereafter   95
           39   To the Press   97
           40   Congratulations and Condolences   102
           41   Thank You   105
           42   Appeals   109
           43   Collecting Correspondence   112
           44   Occasions for Letter-writing   114

Part 5   SUPPLIES, SYSTEMS, STAFF – AND
MODERN TECHNIQUES

Chapter 45   Stationery and Supplies   119
           46   The Outside of the Envelope   120
           47   On Files   121
           48   Notes   122
           49   Abbreviations, Shorthand and Letters to
                Yourself   125
           50   Selling by Mail   127
           51   Secretaries, Dictating Machines – and Other
                Aids   133

52 Your Friend, the Dictating Machine   136
53 Making the Best of Your Secretary and
    Shorthand Typist   139

Part 6 WORD PROCESSING

Chapter 54 Word Processing and Modern Technology
               (by David Roth)   145

Part 7 THE LAW ON LETTERS

Introduction   165
Chapter 55 Copyright   165
           56 Defamation – the Laws of Libel and Slander 169
           57 Sedition, Injurious Falsehood and Other
               Written Traps   171
           58 Affidavits and Oaths   173
           59 The Effect of a Signature   174
           60 Negligence – and Those Who Write Without
               Due Care   176
           61 Liability for the Letters of Your Staff 179
           62 Opening the Mail   181

Part 8 THE LAW IN LETTERS

Introduction   187
Chapter 63 Contracts   187
           64 Restraint Clauses   191
           65 Contracts of Employment   193
           66 Wrongful Dismissal and Unfair Dismissal 195
           67 If You Give No Notice   196

Part 9 LETTERS – AND LITIGATION

Introduction   203
Chapter 68 Letters Before Action – and When Should You
               Sue?   203

69   Litigants, Lawyers and Courts of Law   205
70   Letters in Dispute   208
71   'Without Prejudice'   209
72   Proof of Posting   212

Part 10   APPENDICES

Appendix   1   Post Office Services   217
             2   Abbreviations and Foreign Usage   231
             3   Style – and the Press   235

Index   239

Introduction

Well chosen words in well written letters produce results. Whether the object is increased sales, improved relations with staff, customers, suppliers, or public... action from debtors or inaction from creditors ... the hiring or firing of staff... the granting or refusal of interviews, appointments or posts ... whatever the occasion, the right word means satisfaction, success and money.

Conversely, poor letter-writing costs orders, loses friends and business and destroys profits. The spoken word out of turn may be corrected forthwith. It is ephemeral and fleeting. But words on paper may be used in evidence – and often are.

So the wise executive gives thought and care to the ancient art and craft of the scribe. This book is the executive's guide to profits and everyone's to success, through the written word.

Successful letter-writing means fitting words to occasions. So here are the basic rules on buying and selling, hiring and firing, praising and flattering, sympathising, apologising ... soothing the angry customer, provoking the debtor into payment, cajoling the creditor into compliance ....

Occasions apart, there is another, vital, aspect to letter-writing. This applies whatever the nature of the correspondence. It distinguishes the professional from the amateur, the highly educated from the semi-skilled, the actual or potential top executive from those who will never leave the lower or middle ranks of management. Style is what matters.

As with the manager, salesman, designer, or craftsman, the letterwriter's flair must be inbred. But it can be developed and polished. For instance, there is no excuse for careless grammar, inelegant wording, avoidable commercial clichés or simple bad taste. This book explains how to avoid those stylistic and grammatical pitfalls which mark the letterwriter with the signs of the unschooled, the unpolished, the clumsy, or simply of the ordinary.

So the skilled letterwriter suits style to occasion. But he must also understand the formalities and construction of a fine letter. When, for instance, do you write, 'Dear Mr...' and when should you sign off, 'Yours sincerely'? What are the ideal layouts for letters? Titles matter for men as much as for books. So how do you write to a peer, knight, bishop or judge?

Once your letter is written, you may possibly send it by hand. But the odds are that you will use the postal services. I am grateful to the Post Office for helping me to prepare the appendix on making the best use of the postal services.

Finally, once the letter is written and sent, you want no legal repercussions. So in the section devoted to 'The Law On Letters', you will find the legal rules on defamation (libel and slander) and commercial copyright – and also on those legal subjects most often encountered by the letterwriter, including contracts in general and contracts of employment in particular.

This book was originally *The Businessman's Guide to Letter-Writing and to the Law on Letters,* whose editions were well and happily received – but which have now been outdated, not least by word processors and by the need for modern letterwriters to understand new techniques. So with this book, its predecessor disappears – along with my 'Ewan Mitchell' pen name.

The *Complete Letterwriter* is designed to describe the techniques of efficient and successful letter-writing through a compendium guide to the letterwriter's craft. Should you need specific drafts and precedents, you will find them in companion volumes: *Janner's Handbook of Draft Letters of Employment Law; Janner's Employment Forms;* and (shortly in revised edition) *Janner's Handbook of Boardroom Letters* – all published by Business Books.

Taken separately, this book and the books of drafts each perform different functions. Together, they should provide you with a complete kit and guide to success in what is both an art and a craft. Those who spend (literally) years of working time in writing letters may wish to spare a few hours in what I hope will be a lively study of those rules and principles which can lead to letters which are apt, concise and stylistically suitable, which mark out the writer as a man of executive polish and commercial acumen.

Finally, my warmest thanks to my partner, Mr Paul Secher, LL.B, to my son Daniel Janner, BA(Cantab), barrister, and to my wife for help in the preparation of this book – and to Mr David Roth, for his assistance with the word-processing section.

GREVILLE JANNER

'Dear Madame,

You may wonder why I'm demanding money from you under the threat of violence. Perhaps a few words about myself will help explain matters. I was born to a middle-class family forty-two years ago . . . .

Yours most sincerely . . .'

Part 1

FORM AND FORMALITIES

The Shape of a Letter

A fine letter, like a handsome woman, must have form and shape. For the ordinary, simple note, this creates little worry. By the time you have kicked off with: 'Thank you for your letter . . .' and ended with 'Kindest regards . . .', the middle will look after itself. But where the letter is important; where it matters to you; where you are prepared to take time in working on the words – then you should divide your draft into three parts – the opening, the body and the closing. Create the skeleton in note form; clothe it with the ideas you wish to put across; and the letter takes shape.

The first and last sentences are crucial. Leaving aside any traditional, opening gambit ('We are in receipt of. . .'), you should start a new paragraph with a clear first sentence, to catch the reader's interest . . . to sum up what is to come . . . to make sure that your words will be taken seriously.

Next, each idea should be taken in logical sequence and should lead on, one to the next. Just as each bone of the human body is attached to its fellow, so the ideas in a letter should be jointed. The flow of ideas needs rhythm. Disjointed ideas . . . dislocated thoughts . . . fractured theories . . . these are the hallmark of a poor and ineffective missive.

So jot down the points you wish to make. Then set them out in logical order, so that one flows to the next. Connect them up, if you like, with a general theme. Start with the theme – and then elaborate point by point.

Then round off with the punch line. Explain what action should follow. A good, sound ending to a well constructed letter should bring business or results or whatever other object for which the writing is intended. If the skeleton of a letter is sound, then even if the body is not as strong as it might be, there is an excellent chance that the reader will not notice. But ignore the skeleton and the odds are that your letter will prove a rambling disaster.

Hail and Farewell – for the
Start and Finish of a Letter

A bad beginning or an inadequate end spoils any letter. Happily, the formalities dictated by usage and etiquette do much to ease the writer's path – provided that he gets them right.

However much you may dislike the recipient of your letter, there is seldom any alternative to calling him 'Dear'. To commence: 'Hated Sir' is unthinkable. To leave out the 'Dear' altogether is about as far as hostility (or formality) can decently go. Generally, this opening denotes hostility implacable . . . indignation unquenchable . . . It has a somewhat antique and Victorian ring about it and should seldom be used, except in official (and probably governmental) traditional notifications.

The use of a person's name, without the opening endearment, is generally only suitable for inter-office memos – or letters written to ex-partners or associates. 'Jackson: I can no longer endure working with you . . .' In practice, this approach is best reserved for epistles to one's spouse – which, of course, may (one hopes) begin: 'Darling . . . .'

What really matters is to get the name right, once you use it. If you have not taken the trouble to ascertain the spelling of your correspondent's surname, you can hardly blame him if he feels that you are not really concerned with his business. We are all inordinately sensitive to our names – they represent ourselves. Not for nothing do political hotheads disfigure the names of their enemies, on signs, posters and hoardings. You may paint a moustache or a beard on to the poster portrait, out of fun – but to destroy a man's image is a gesture of contempt.

To make an error in a person's name is normally a sign of nothing but carelessness, and carelessness is hardly a good advertisement for you, your wares or services. If in doubt, check, or get your secretary to do so. If the name is incorrect, it will have escaped both you and your secretary – double negligence, visible to all. A telephone call to the recipient's secretary (or even telephonist) would have put things right. Is his name Philip with one 'l' or two? Is he 'Goldsmith' or 'Goldschmidt' or, for that matter, 'Goldshmidt'? Is he 'Mr Ewan Richard' or 'Mr Evan Richards', 'Mr Harald Stewart' or 'Mr Harold Stuart'?

When writing to a woman, try to address her correctly as 'Mrs' or 'Miss'. If in doubt, 'Ms' avoids disaster. And some women see no reason why their marital status should be revealed in their form of address, any more than it is for a man – so they regard 'Ms' as a feminist entitlement.

Of course 'Dear Madam' (with an 'e' at the end, only when writing to a French lady, the wife of an ambassador or possibly to a brothel proprietress) solves the problem – in the same way as 'Dear Sir' or 'Dear Sirs'. But it is a very formal approach, and should generally be reserved for strictly formal letters, including those written to public bodies as such, as opposed to specific individuals within them. If you wish to deal with a person on a personal basis, then use his name.

Whether or not to address a man by his first (or 'given' or Christian) name is usually a matter of tact, dependent upon your acquaintance or friendship with him. On the other hand, it is often a mistake to be 'too chummy' – but if you can get on first-name terms with business contacts, then (in most cases) you will reduce the fences between you. There are other occasions when 'keeping your distance' may be an advantage. The letterwriter must judge this problem for himself.

What, then, of the word 'my'? 'My Dear James . . . ' 'My Dear Brown . . . . '

This approach should be used with care. It is consistently employed by the upper crust to express warmth – but is sometimes taken by others to imply condescension. Custom differs, but if in doubt, leave off the 'my'.

When addressing the recipient by his own name (surname or first name as the case may be), the almost invariable sign-off is 'Yours sincerely'. 'Yours very sincerely' is in order, if a little flowery. 'Yours ever' should be reserved for good friends. 'Yours truly' is a useful variation, to be used together with the surname introduction, where the recipient is not well known to the writer.

'Yours faithfully' is the appropriate ending to a letter commencing 'Dear Sir'. It has almost entirely replaced the old-fashioned, 'I remain, your obedient servant', which is nowadays largely confined to the military.

Reversing the order of final words is sometimes done but usually regarded as an affectation. 'Faithfully yours' or 'Very sincerely yours' are a rarity. Between friends, 'Yours' on its own is common. 'As ever' or again 'Yours ever' do good service. 'Sincerely' adds a touch of goodwill. But all these are variations on the basic themes of: 'Dear Sir . . . Yours faithfully' and 'Dear Mr Brown . . . Yours sincerely', and come into the small minority of penned letters. As I said: stick to the formalities and you are likely to start and finish correctly. You can then concentrate on the body of the letter that comes in between them.

3

Signatures and Postscripts

There are people who make their living through interpreting character as expressed in signatures. Loops, whirls and lines, we are told, all have hidden meanings. Slope the words downwards and you are likely to be depressed and pessimistic; slope them up and the graphologist recognises an extroverted optimist. Whether this has any scientific foundation is arguable (and often argued). But the importance of a sensible signature is beyond dispute.

Your signature is your symbol. How do you make it? The height of modesty is to use an initial only: 'N. Smith'. Next in the scale of self assertion, the forename and surname: 'Norman Smith'. Then comes the initial: 'Norman H. Smith'. Finally and most flourishing: 'Norman Halliwell Smith'.

Which signature will impress most depends upon the nature of the letter. Suppose for instance, the writer wants a job as salesman. The more extroverted he manages to appear, the more likely it is that he will get the post. Conversely, if a director is seeking a self-effacing assistant, he should look for the man with the quiet initials.

Finally, if you have to sign dozens of letters a day, you should develop a characteristic scrawl which enables you to fix your imprimatur with the minimum expenditure of time and effort. But any self-assured and swift symbol that impresses your staff or your regular correspondents may ruin the object of your letter if the recipient expects you to treat him with careful, considered respect. If you receive an application for an executive position, signed with a swirl and a squiggle, would you be impressed? Hardly. Then remember that, next time *you* decide to switch boardrooms.

A prominent businessman who enlivens his speech with aphorisms likes to say: 'A businessman's mind should be like a chemist's shop. A place for everything and everything in its place.' Again: 'A tidy mind in a tidy body – that is the recipe for success.' Laugh if you like, but there are few who appreciate untidiness. And if a signature is slovenly, then (rightly or wrongly) its reader may draw a fairly obvious conclusion about the signatory.

In former days, traders and merchants took great pride in their seals. If they needed to sign, they pressed their ring or sealing rod or cylinder on to the wax and they made their mark. Today, alas, the handsome, chiselled seal is gone. Your mark is your signature. It puts the final touches on your letters. So ensure that the touch is firm, appropriate and impressive. Many a good letter brings bad results because the writer is too lazy or too thoughtless to add a fine, smart signature, suited to the nature and design of the words it rounds off.

If you go abroad on business, you will check your luggage before you go. Forget your underwear or your outerwear and you will have to buy more. In letter-writing, too, care pays dividends. In particular: before you sign your letter, do make sure that it includes everything that you have in mind. A PS may help, but afterthoughts are too obvious.

Omissions may be corrected either through the re-writing of the letter itself or by a striking out or by the addition of a PS – which may be typed or handwritten. But anything added by hand should be transposed to the carbon copy if it has any potential importance. So spare time to read your letters, quietly and carefully, before you sign them.

There is nothing wrong in getting your secretary to put at the foot: 'Dictated by Mr James Jones but signed in his absence', or simply: 'Diane Williams, pp James Jones'. Provided your correspondent will not be offended, all is well, but do make certain that the words for which you will be held responsible are accurate. And you might even say: 'I hope that you will not mind this letter being signed in my absence, by my secretary, so as to save a day – I am away tomorrow, in the North . . . . '

If this happens often, then why not invest in a battery of those excellent stamps which give your secretary the choice between the different forms of 'pp' 'sign-offs'. Warning: please do not, repeat *not*, allow your secretary or anyone else to sign a letter with your signature and without your approval – other than in the rarest cases and when you have the most magnificent and reliable pro-signatory.

Robert Browning, praising the glories of England in April, extolled 'the wise thrush, who sings his song twice over'. It is enough for the wise letterwriter to read his words once over – providing that he does so with care.

Far too many letters receive a scrawled signature, in great haste, at the end of the day. If you are guilty of this sort of slovenliness, then at least realise what you are leaving undone.

4

Lists and Schedules

Essentially, a letter is a vehicle for ideas. Dry fact is better contained in an enclosure or appendix. 'Full details are enclosed herewith . . . .' Or: 'Particulars are attached . . .'.

In general, a letter is intended to be read. If the recipient is too bored or aggravated to read to the end, then the letter has failed – it was carelessly drafted, poorly written, badly typed or simply inept, inadequate or unfitted for its purpose.

Lists or schedules are (usually, at least) intended to be consulted, perused, dipped into, extracted from . . . .

Unless the letter is apt, the list or schedule will prove useless. The letter sells the writer's ideas – and often his goods or services. It requires serious consideration. But the form and content of the schedule require thought, too. However good your opening gambit, if you cannot checkmate your opponent, you lose the game.

So if you want your enclosures to bear good fruit, you should fertilise them with your time, care and consideration. You have no time to spare? Then at least make sure that someone else does so for you. Your enclosures should neither be nor appear to be afterthoughts – in the true meaning of that word.

There are some lists that fit well into the body of the letter. If you are setting out a string of thoughts, then by all means do so in numbered turn. Thus:

Our reasons are the following:
(a) The product is too new.
(b) The area is too limited.
(c) . . . .

Alternatively:

We are sure that you will appreciate the reductions in prices in the following products:
(a) . . . .

and so on.

Not for nothing do we talk of 'enlisting' someone's help. Lists can make a letter live. Pack your facts or arguments all together into a paragraph and you may succeed in confusing both the opposition and yourself. List your thoughts in what you think is a logical order and if, on reading them through, logic is missing then *you* will know – and redraft your letter, recast your list or change your mind accordingly.

Finally, do remember to refer to the enclosure not only in the letter itself but at its foot. The word 'enclosure' typed in red should do the trick. Alternatively, staple the letter to the accompanying documents so that they cannot go adrift. For every letter that gets lost, there must be fifty missing enclosures – which means loss to the writer and (if he retains his interest and applies for copies) aggravation for the recipient. So make sure that both letter and enclosure both go and stick together.

5

References – on Letters

References are as important for letters as they are for people. Careful, sensible, thoughtful referencing saves hours of work – and hence time and money. It enables the recipient of your letters to know what you are referring to, so avoiding mistakes and also showing that you are a courteous correspondent. It also enables your own filing system to operate efficiently.

Every business letter should bear a general reference, after the opening or at the top of the page:

Dear Sir,
Your Order No. 25873

Or:

Dear Sir,
Directors' Loan Account

If you initiate the correspondence, you can generally choose the main reference. Try to make it specific (where possible, for instance, referring to an order or contract by a number, or a person by his full name rather than by surname alone). The more careful and precise your reference, the greater its use for you.

If the correspondence is commenced by the other party, the chances are that you will have his reference – which you will repeat on your reply. But do not hesitate to add a reference of your own, if necessary.

The subject matter gets set out in the general reference. But the identity of the writer and typist should also be indicated.

There are two ways of achieving this. Most commonly, you will put the initials of each. But if you would prefer to remain anonymous, you can allocate numbers or letters to each executive and typist in the organisation. If anyone wants to find out the identity of a person whose initials are on the notepaper, all he usually has to do is to telephone the business number and ask. But where the letter is deliberately anonymous (as in some debt-collecting missives) it may be preferable to include a reference which is clear to you but meaningless to your correspondents.

Obviously, copies of all-important correspondence will be kept and filed (see Chapter 47). The filing may be done by a secretary of high intellect – but this would probably be a waste of her good (and expensive) time. More likely (or more profitably) you will employ a filing clerk, or put the office junior on to the filing chore as part of his daily routine. You must then recognise the limitations of your employee, and cater for them. If you want the copy to be readily available, it must appear on the right file. So your referencing must be precise, clear and individual. The whole subject is worth a few minutes of careful thought now, so as to avoid wasted hours and energy in the future.

6

The Layout of a Letter

Well marshalled thoughts, set out in well chosen words, may still convey the wrong impression if the letter is carelessly laid out. So instruct your secretary and typists in the layout you require.

You may decide on some special, house style. Eccentricity may be your line. There are millionaires who slouch around in baggy trousers, multi-coloured neckties and without a penny in their pockets. I treasure letters from a great foreign statesman containing torrents of thought, poured out on the scruffiest of paper and entirely without paragraphs. The mighty are entitled to their foibles.

For the average, successful executive – or for the man who aspires to even higher levels in the commercial world – more prosaic behaviour is advisable. Once you are chairman, if your finger-nails are dirty this will perhaps be regarded as one of the amusing but forgivable ways of 'the Old Man', who has better things to do than to attend to his toilet. If you are the majority shareholder as well as managing director, then your notepaper can be scruffy and if anyone minds, that is just too bad. But if you are lower down the line – or, in most cases, if you wish to stay at the top of the heap – then appearance matters.

The executive generally realises the importance of being well groomed. He may even appreciate that his stationery should be as well turned out as his person. It is remarkable, though, how many men at the top take too little care over the layout of their letters.

Eccentricities on one side, I recommend a standard style. Across the top of the letter goes your heading. On one side (it matters not which) comes your address – probably with the date underneath it. Slightly lower down and preferably on the opposite side we have the recipient's address. The date fits in where it balances best.

Then: 'Dear Sir' (or as the case may be) goes hard against the left margin. Margins on each side should be adequate, both so as to give a sense of space to the letter and to allow marginal notes as required by the recipient.

Typing should be double spaced, with treble spacing between paragraphs – the start of which should be indented. Sub-paragraphs require further indentation. Finally, the sign-off comes towards the middle of the page; there must be adequate space for the signature. Underneath comes the name of the writer, and underneath that his style or position.

If there are enclosures, add the word: 'Enclosure' (or the abbreviation 'Encl.') at the bottom right-hand corner, preferably in red (see Chapter 4). If you cannot complete your message on one page, use a continuation sheet, rather than the back of the paper. All stationery ordered should come with continuation sheets of the same size and of identical paper.

Finally, remember the reference (see Chapter 34). Normally, this is best placed somewhere at the top.

Here is a suggested layout:

The Jamestown Plc
24 High Street, Jamesville, Beds

Ref: GJ23   1 September 1983

Roger Brown & Co. Ltd,
38 Upper Street,
Millbury, Wilts.

Dear Sirs,
We thank you for your letter of 30 August. We shall be pleased to supply the goods required, if you will kindly provide the following further information:

(a)
(b)
(c)

We look forward to an early reply and will do our best to despatch the goods immediately we receive your further instructions.

Yours faithfully,

Director

7

Acknowledgements –
and Standard Forms*

The surest way to lose friends and have no influence on other people is not to reply to their letters.

Part of the art of ensuring prompt replies lies in an efficient office system. Are you satisfied that yours is as good as you can make it? Is incoming mail stamped with a date and shipped off smartly to the

*See also Part 6 on word processing.

appropriate department? Does a letter requiring an immediate answer always get one? If there is to be delay, then do you send the appropriate acknowledgement?

'We thank you for your letter of . . ., which is receiving attention.' *Alternatively:* 'We are obliged to you for your esteemed order. We shall deal with this as soon as possible.' *Or:* 'Your communication is acknowledged. A reply will be sent shortly.' *Or:* 'We are in receipt of your letter of . . . . This has been passed to . . . for his attention.'

What you really need is a batch of assorted acknowledgements, to be sent out as required. With luck, you will have someone to sort out the mail who is capable of deciding which acknowledgement would be appropriate. Otherwise, it does not take a genius at a slightly higher level to deal with the mail by sorting it into the appropriate tray, to allocate the necessary card, or to say to a secretary: 'Form 1 for this, please . . . . Form 2 for that . . . '

Standard forms there must be. These can be simple, brief and on postcards. Or circumstances may require something lengthier. For example, you may wish to set out a series of possible, common answers to a communication, all but one or two of which can be crossed out. Examples:

We regret that we have not received the order to which you refer. Would you kindly send a copy so that the matter may be dealt with as quickly as possible.

We are obliged to you for your order, but you do not stipulate an address for delivery. If you would kindly do so, the goods will be despatched within . . . days/weeks/months.

We regret that it is not possible to despatch orders overseas.

We regret that the lines which you have ordered are for export only. We are sorry that we cannot be of assistance on this occasion.

The goods the subject matter of your esteemed order have been sent to you by post/air/sea. They should reach you by about . . . . If they are not received by then, kindly contact us again.

We have checked our records. These indicate that the goods were despatched to you. We regret that they appear to have been lost in the post. We will send replacements/without extra charge/investigate the matter/contact our carriers forthwith.

Unfortunately, we are not able to open accounts for small amounts. If you will kindly send a cheque or postal order, we shall despatch at once.

Naturally, you may wish to add a standard PS: 'We have pleasure in enclosing herewith our latest catalogue, which we hope will be of interest to you.' *Or:* 'In case our other products may be of interest to you, we are despatching an up-to-date catalogue and price list under separate cover.' *Or:* 'It has been a pleasure to do business with you. We shall send you further details of new lines from time to time.'

It is, of course, important that even *pro forma* letters should be well laid out (see Chapter 6), and properly produced. You may have facilities for printing on your premises. You may decide to use a duplicating machine. There is a tremendous variety of magnificent modern machinery on the market, tailored to suit almost every commercial pocket (details in Part 6). Before you take the plunge, make sure that servicing and spares will be available. Keep your eyes on the journals, sent out (often to a controlled circulation and entirely free), and aimed at potential buyers of equipment. If you are not on the various mailing lists, then ask your secretary to make a few phone calls and get yourself added. For details of current publications, you could look at the *Annual Press Directory,* which is in every comprehensive reference library. Or ask one of your business friends to pass over the journals he gets.

Of course, the nature and variety of the forms which you will have in stock will vary according to your business. You may find it helpful to prepare a book of forms, to be adapted. Many of them should be available in large numbers and will not warrant individual typing. You will find hundreds of draft precedents in my companion volumes to this.

To avoid duplication, I have omitted from this book any detailed advice and precedents on (for instance) letters to debtors. But the sort of standard draft you will require is this:

Dear Sir,
We regret that your account remains outstanding, in spite of several reminders. In order to avoid any unpleasantness, we trust that you will now forward your remittance without further delay.
Yours faithfully,

Or:

Dear Sir,
You leave us with no alternative. Your debt will be placed in the hands of our solicitors for their immediate attention, unless your remittance is received by return of post.
Yours faithfully,

In my companion volumes, then, there are many draft letters, designed to get you in your money without actually taking legal proceedings. Again, a chapter and an appendix are devoted to letters to your bank. The drafts have been carefully tailored with the help of a brilliant bank manager, now retired. So 'letters to your bank manager' are not included in this book. But the greater your need for credit, the more careful you must be in handling the man who handles your (actual or potential) overdraft.

'I shall not want to duplicate letters to my own bank manager', you protest.

Precisely. You will need to draft them with care; to make use of available precedents; but you will not use printed or duplicated forms. The sauce for the goose indebted to you is not the sauce also for the gander to whom you owe money.

What is required, then, is careful organisation of your letter-writing system. Work out those letters which can be reproduced, by whatever method is most appropriate. Forms can save a vast amount of time and money. Set on one side the letters which are sufficiently standard for the use of draft precedents – and use those precedents to lean on. If you do not wish to invest in a collection of other people's drafts, then prepare one of your own. And leave for individual drafting only those letters which require individual thought and attention.

So you need a system for sorting out your correspondence and dealing with it. With the sole and rare exception of those letters which you deliberately ignore, all must be acknowledged.

8

Names and Titles

Do you call your correspondent by his surname – or 'Mr' – or what if he has a title?

Consider first the use of the surname only. 'Dear Brown . . . ' This comes at both ends of the social scale. Many Public School boys could well have been born without any Christian names at all. Like certain stars of stage and screen (Fernandel and Topol, for instance) they are addressed by surname only. It remains a sign of intimacy to write to them by their surnames, even in later life.

Ministers, Members of Parliament and barristers never use the prefix 'Mr' (nor 'Mrs' or 'Miss', for that matter) when addressing a colleague. If the person is not sufficiently well known to them to be addressed by their Christian name, then the surname it is. This sort of approach is quite acceptable in sections of the upper-level world of commerce.

Some employers keep their staff at a distance by addressing them by their surnames. Call it an army hangover, if you will, but the boss may refer to Mr Arthur Brown as 'Brown', without offence being taken. The chances are, in those cases, that employees so named will be expected to address the person who sees fit not to call them 'Mr', as 'Sir'.

One well known barrister's clerk who had held a high rank in the army and found himself back in The Temple was required to address even the most callow, new arrival at the Bar as 'Sir', and retaliated by addressing everyone as 'Sir', including fellow clerks, ushers in the courts and other gentlemen who would not normally be accorded that dignity. The French do it, do they not? And so has he – ever since.

My advice? If in doubt, call the man 'Mr'. The days when it was appropriate to talk down to employees have long since passed. If you place them on the same level as yourself, then resentment is far less likely to arise. In your particular position or company or area, the tradition may still be to call a man by his surname alone. Well and good. But if in doubt, give the man his title.

The most common title (apart from a military or police rank) is that of 'Sir'. This is accorded to Knights and Baronets of various orders and degrees. In each case, unless you are on first-name terms with them, the correct form of address is: 'Dear Sir Arthur . . .', 'Dear Sir Barnett . . .' or as the case may be. But never 'Dear Sir Jones'.

The situation with Ladies (by title as well as in behaviour) is rather different. The wife of a Knight or Baronet is called 'Lady Jane Jones', so you would write to her: 'Dear Jane' if you know her well enough – or otherwise, 'Dear Lady Jones'. The same applies if she is the wife of Lord Jones.

If the lady has a title in her own right, then you can address her as 'Dear Lady Jones' or 'Dear Baroness Jones' (or, if you are on friendly but not first-name terms, 'My Dear Baroness'. 'Dear Baroness' is unusual).

The exception to the use of the surname for the lady occurs where she is the daughter of a viscount, earl, marquis or duke. She is then accorded the courtesy title of 'Lady Jane Jones' – so you write to her as 'Dear Lady Jane'.

The children of all peers (life or hereditary) have the courtesy title of 'The Honourable'. But you still write to them as 'Dear Mr . . .' and never as 'Dear Honourable Jones'. In practice, the courtesy title is on its way out and is seldom used by most of its possessors.

The lady with the female equivalent of a Knighthood is a 'Dame'. She is not addressed as 'Lady' but as 'Dame'. And, like a Knight, it is combined with her Christian and not her surname. Hence: 'Dear Dame Jane . . .' and *not* 'Dear Dame Jones . . .'.

The highest rank before the peerage is that of baronet. On the envelope he is called: 'Sir James Jones, Bt.' – but the 'Bt.' is never used when addressing the gentleman. Equally, the lowest rank of the peerage is that of the baron. While, as we have seen, baronesses are often addressed by their title, the same does not apply to barons. They are always called 'Lord'. Hence: 'Dear Lord Jones.'

Higher up the lordly scale, you could either write 'Dear Viscount Jones' or 'Dear Lord Jones' – either would do. The same applies to earls, marquises and dukes.

The wife of duke is a duchess; of a marquis, a marchioness; of an earl, a countess; of a viscount, a viscountess. Write to them either as: 'Dear Lady Jones' or 'Dear Countess Jones' – but just as you write to a duke as 'Your Grace', the same dignity is accorded to his wife. Never write: 'Dear Duchess Jones'.

What, then, of the gentleman of the cloth? 'Dear Reverend Jones'; 'Dear Father Jones'; or 'Dear Monsignor Jones' or (even) 'Dear Rabbi Jones' – all these are fine. For Archbishop Jones: 'Dear Archbishop' (informally) or 'Your Grace', when you know him not.

The formal sign-off would be 'I remain, your obedient servant' – but 'Yours faithfully', 'Yours truly' and 'Yours sincerely' are much more common, unless the occasion is highly formal.

Archbishops are generally addressed as: 'His Grace the Lord Archbishop of . . .'. To a bishop, write: 'The Right Reverend the Lord Bishop of . . .' or 'The Lord Bishop of . . .'. Start your letter: 'My Lord Bishop' or 'Your Lordship'.

Catholic dignitaries generally receive the same courtesies as their Protestant brethren. The following guide is suggested:

When writing to a Cardinal, address the envelop: 'His Eminence the Cardinal Archbishop of . . .'. Address him as 'Your Eminence' or

'My Lord Cardinal'. To a Catholic Bishop: 'His Lordship the Bishop of . . . '. Address him as 'My Lord'. And to a Catholic priest: 'The Reverend . . . '. Start the letter 'Dear Father . . . '.

The Chief Rabbi should be addressed as: 'The Very Reverend the Chief Rabbi'. Start your letter: 'Dear Chief Rabbi'. Otherwise, Rabbis get addressed as 'Rabbi Michael Cohen', or 'Rabbi Dr Michael Cohen' (as the case may be). Start: 'Dear Rabbi Cohen'. A Jewish minister who does not hold a rabbinical diploma is normally: 'The Reverend Michael Cohen'. Start: 'Dear Reverend Cohen' or 'Dear Mr Cohen'.

Now, the law. Know a judge well and call him by his first name. Know him reasonably well (but not on first-name terms) and address him as 'Sir William' or 'Judge Jones' (according to rank).

Writing to the Lord Chancellor? Address: 'The Right Honourable The Lord Chancellor'. Write: 'My Lord'. Similarly to Lords of Appeal in Ordinary and to the Lord Chief Justice.

To the Master of the Rolls, address: 'To the Right Honourable Lord . . . ', or 'To the Right Honourable Sir . . . ', Master of the Rolls. Alternatively: 'His Honour, The Master of the Rolls'.

Lord Justices of Appeal? Superscribe: 'The Right Honourable, the Lord Justice . . . ', or 'The Right Honourable Sir William . . . , Lord Justice of Appeal'. Write: 'Sir'.

Lord Mayors? 'The Right Honourable the Lord Mayor of . . . '. Write 'My Lord . . .'. An ordinary mayor is: 'His Worship, the Mayor of . . .'. 'Your Worship . . .'.

Address a Member of Parliament as: 'Roger Smith Esq., MP' or, as 'Esq.' is disappearing, 'Roger Smith, MP' is fine. If he is a Privy Councillor, he is 'The Right Honourable Roger Smith, MP'. In either case, start: 'Dear Sir' or 'Dear Mr Smith'.

Doctors of Medicine? 'Dr Roger Smith.' But note: surgeons are 'Mr'. Hence: 'Roger Smith Esq., FRCS . . . Dear Mr Smith . . . '.

Writing to a commissioned officer in one of the armed services? Address him by rank, together with decorations if he has any. If he is a Lieutenant Colonel, write: 'Dear Colonel . . . ' and *never* 'Dear Lt-Col. . . . '. You may add the arm of service to the title of army officers and 'RN' to the address of naval officers.

On a more plebian level, address a female as 'Dear Madam', but *not* 'Dear Miss' nor (still less) 'My dear Ms'. The old-fashioned 'Master Jones' for a young boy is on its way out.

Difficulties arise when writing to more than one person. Some say that a letter should be addressed to one person only. But most think that 'Dear Mr and Mrs Jones' is appropriate. Leave out their degrees and the like. If you write to Sir James Smith, MP – all is well. But you omit the 'MP' when writing to Sir James and Lady Smith.

Call two or more married women: 'Mesdames', and two or more spinsters: 'The Misses . . . '. Some say that if you write to two or more business women, you can start your letter: 'Ladies . . . '.

These are general rules. If you are ever in doubt, get your secretary to telephone the secretary of the person to whom you are writing. 'How does he like to be addressed, please?' You will soon find out the answer – which will avoid creating quite unnecessary ill-will. People are very touchy about their forms of title and address. Courtesy requires that you address your correspondent with all due care.

'Pretty stylish set of references I have there, eh Mr. Bradley?'

Part 2

STYLE AND GRAMMAR

Style

You judge an applicant for a job by his clothes, his appearance, and by his manner of speech or writing – in a word, by his style. First impressions may be vital – so style may be crucial. *If* you get to know the man, then other factors come into play – his character and intellect, in particular. But at first, it is his outward style that matters. If that is poor, then he may get no chance to show that his gauche exterior conceals a mind of gold.

The would-be employee (at whatever level) who turns up for interview poorly turned out is likely to be put out – in both senses of that term. The potential executive with dirty finger-nails may have potential which is outstanding – but the odds are that he will stand outside.

Equally, the letterwriter must pay heed to the immediate impact of his correspondence. This means careful attention to stationery and printing (see Chapter 45), to cleanliness of type and to skill of typist (see Chapter 53). It also requires that the words themselves have an immediate impact.

An illiterate letter should be a contradiction in terms. Grammar matters (see Chapter 10). If the writer is uneducated, unless precedents are used and adapted with loving care, the reader will know. (The best, permanent answer is for the writer to become a reader himself – do you take pride in your library? The first stage to correction is recognition of failings. If the writer can achieve this on his own, then well and good. Otherwise, why is there such a prejudice against formal education in letter-writing and literature generally?)

Style, of course, cannot be detached from general layout. The letterwriter, like the athlete, must get his start and his finish just right if his effort is to produce a winner. The contents must be clear, brief and lucid – and pleasantly paragraphed (Chapter 12). But above all, the style of the words must reflect the intention of the letter itself.

A morning suit may be a winner for the races or ideal at the wedding – but would black or grey best suit the occasion? Going out for the evening? Then do you wear a dinner-jacket – and does your wife appear in long or short evening-dress? A lawyer must wear a dark suit in court – no problem there – but what do you wear when you greet the executive from abroad at your club? Dress must suit occasion or it may cause embarrassment, upset, loss of business – as we said, first impressions matter and they are created by dress. Women realise this far more than men and give much greater attention to their garb. If the female of the species appears a fool, this is generally by design.

The words of the letterwriter are the dress of his thoughts. If they are inept, slovenly, ill-suited to the occasion, then their style will destroy their impact. Conversely, fit the style to the circumstance and all should be well.

So now consider some stylistic occasions.

10

Grammatical Thoughts, Ungrammatical Words – and Adult Remedies

'Between you and I', the letter begins . . . . If the reader is a purist, the correspondence ends. If the writer is an applicant for a job, his prospects pall. Instead of achieving a confidential approach, he has revealed his lack of understanding of elementary English grammar.

Again: 'I am obliged to you for the courtesy extended to Mr Brown and I, on our recent visit to your factory'. Courtesy extended to I?

'My staff and me are grateful . . . '. So 'me' is grateful, is me? Someone does not understand the use of the accusative. He is a self-accused and self-confessed murderer of the English tongue. He is guilty of a very common crime.

When you write letters, your accent disappears. Your speech may bear the marks of Belgravia or Bohemia, Brooklyn or Bermondsey but your writing receives no overtones from your voice. This may be a great asset. Like it or not, the commercial world is snob-ridden and class-controlled. Speak your mind in the Queen's English and you are generally better off than to pronounce your thoughts in Cotswold or Cockney. But on paper, every man starts on the same level. Pens and typewriters are classless instruments. The heavily accented words which you speak into your dictating machine emerge classless, sexless and without indication of ethnic or racial origin. At least, they should.

In practice, grammar tends to be the giveaway. It places the seal of education on the letter of authority. Conversely, if ungrammatically worded, the writer stands revealed as an uneducated person. Not for nothing do we use the words 'unlettered' and 'illiterate' for those whose education is lacking.

Now, we are not all blessed with equal opportunity in our early years. Some of the top men of commerce were forced out into the business world at a very early age. But once there, most of them read widely and improved themselves (in the best sense of that phrase). Good companies buy good books if they wish to have excellent executives. Wise workers with mind and pen recognise their own deficiencies in education.

What can be done, then, to repair broken English? I have three suggestions.

First, read well and widely. By all means study the financial columns in the newspapers and the form of both companies and race horses. But fill in those odd moments on the train, bus, in the car or taxi by reading something better. Have you dipped into Hersey or Hemmingway? Do you really think that David Copperfield was a character in a film? Have you relived those memorable years in the words of Winston Churchill? What of Solzhenitzyn?

Schools all too often spell 'literature' with a capital 'L'. They sate the appetite for Shakespeare by turning the words of the unfortunate Bard into examination fodder. A pity. To write well you should read widely – and the greater your failings as a grammarian, the more you should soak your mind in the rich wine of fine literature. There we have it again – 'literature' – the art of letters . . . the skills of the literate . . . the letterwriter who wishes his words to carry impact should read the letters of others.

Incidentally, you may take this suggestion literally, if you wish. Many of the greatest men have consigned their thoughts to letters. Bernard Shaw and countless others have caused or permitted their letters to be published. Read them.

Second, listen to good speech. By all means treat yourself to Sir Winston Churchill records, if you are feeling flush (or maybe there is a record library in your area?). On a more prosaic level, when you hear the language well spoken, make a mental note. To copy the excellent is a mark of wisdom.

Finally, do not turn up your nose at formal courses, aimed at adults. If you do not wish to attend a class, then have one custom-made – get yourself a teacher. The money will be well spent. Try correspondence courses, if you like – there are plenty about. Never mind the cost. It pays to learn. It is never too late to acquire polish. And while your tutors may have to advertise their services, there is no need for you to advertise that you are making use of them.

11

Punctuation, Self-expression – and the Limits to Formal Grammar

The object of a letter is to propound an idea. Whether you are buying or selling, hiring or firing, praising, decrying, apologising, negotiating . . . it matters not. You are enagaging in self-expression, on paper. As we shall see in Chapter 16, there are occasions when formality is helpful, to keep the self hidden. But generally, what matters is to say what you must (or what you wish) with clarity. And at the same time, it is your personality that needs expression, along with your views.

To this end, formal grammar has its place. Sentences, we are told at school, must have verbs. Not necessarily. A sentence usually has a verb. But not always. Modern writing need not follow infant lines. Classical form has its place in ballet, but so does free expression, found in the dancers' work of today. Everything depends upon the work to be interpreted, the music to be followed, the story the artistes seek to portray.

So it is with letters. There is a place for the traditional style of the formal work – and for the untraditional, thrusting, vivid writing of the informal thought. So be not afraid of the lively phrase. Words may make a sentence, with no verb at all. So may one word, on its own. Often. And effectively.

In general, sentences should not begin with 'And'. But they often do. And to good effect. You are the writer. You make your own rules. Yours is the meaning to be expressed, the personality to be put across, the style to be chosen.

Or take punctuation. The full stop is called in pungent American, the 'period'. It indicates a break in the thought. A comma marks a pause. A semicolon is half a colon – and is useful for indicating the end of an item in a list. The colon comes between the semicolon and the full stop: we have a pause in the flow of thought, but not for long. It is also used a great deal nowadays before quotation marks, thus: 'We undertake that the goods will be delivered by the end of next week', you write – those were the words used.

The dash is a useful weapon – the pause is pregnant ... the break in the sentence (or in the list) longer than the mere series of dots.... The dots themselves show that the thought has not ended, even though the sentence or the paragraph may have done.

Careful punctuation breaks up a paragraph or a sentence. The breezier the style you choose to adopt, the more use you will make of the dot and the dash, the colon and the semicolon.

So to suit the style to the subject and to the writer means far more than the careful choice of words. They must be strung into the appropriate phrases or sentences and linked or divided by appropriate punctuation.

Modern usage often justifies the ignoring of ancient rules. Take the split infinitive, for example. As far as I am concerned, you should keep it to yourself. This is a matter of taste. To carefully fix ... to gently remind ... to kindly honour ... to swiftly reply ... to eagerly await ... to please reply ... no doubt these are all entirely proper. But we all have our linguistic foibles. I am in favour of the splitting of the atom for peaceful purposes, but cringe at the splitting of the infinitive for any purpose whatsoever.

No doubt this is entirely wrong, old fashioned and stupid. I can only suggest that, before you split your infinitives in your letters, you might bear in mind that it is just possible that the recipient of your letter – who may, perhaps, be an important customer (actual or potential) or someone else whom you wish to please – may be equally wrong, old-fashioned and stupid. You may often please yourself about modern grammar. But if you fail to please your correspondent, you would probably have been better off not to have corresponded at all. You would not deliberately offend, say, a potential customer in speech. Then do not do so in writing. He is entitled to his views as you are to yours. Even with grammar, tact plays its part.

12

Brevity

Those of us who are small in physical stature are often reassured by kindly, witty friends who say: 'The best things come in small packages . . . a little person is a beautiful thing . . . it's the size of the brain that counts . . . ' and so on. For the man who craves that extra foot so as to become world high-jump champion, or the woman who has to speak in public, resting her chin on the table, these pithy thoughts provide small consolation. But they do contain a germ of truth. Size is all very well in its way – but it may be a nuisance. The tall man cannot stretch out in the bath nor extend his legs in the sleeper or couchette. He can peer over the top of the crowd but seldom slide through it. As with people, so with letters.

There are times when a letter must be long in order to achieve its purpose. But generally, the shorter the words, the sentences and the letter, the more effective the result. Even the longest epistle should be broken up into brief sections. There is no excuse whatsoever for the sentence that stretches into a paragraph nor the paragraph into a page.

Brevity is the soul of a good letter. Short, snappy, concise, clear and pungent paragraphs. Thoughts neatly packed into words with punch. Neat, lively expressions, shorn of padding and pomposity. These are the keys to successful correspondence. The bore, the wind-bag, the man whom we would all go the longest distance to avoid – he is the lonely denizen of the bar or the club – but he is also the writer whose letters we least like to read. 'Oh, him again', you say, recognising with a groan, the prolix prose. 'I'll read it later . . . that is, if I have time . . . ', and so the writer joins the great unread.

In the world of journalism, there are papers that pay by the word or column inch. This puts a premium on padding and there are many professional writers (this author included) who do their very best to avoid this sort of yardstick. 'We only want 500 words', writes the editor. 'We pay £X per thousand.' 'I shall be delighted to write your piece', the journalist replies. 'But it will be harder for me to condense the material you want into 500 words than to produce a piece of 1,000. I respectfully suggest that it would be fairer to pay the rate of £X for the 500-word piece. It will take me longer to write and will cost infinitely more in care.' With luck, the editor will agree – as a professional himself he will know that length and value are seldom the same. Quality counts. Brevity matters.

In the world of the public speaker, there is a trite saying 'Stand up, speak up and then shut up'. Again: 'If you can't strike oil in five minutes, stop boring'. But at least the speaker's words are transitory. Unless you happen to be the President of the United States or a politician who produces some glorious gaffe – or unless, of course, you slander in speech – the chances are that your words will go unrecorded and, in the long run at least, unremembered. But the commercial correspondent will have his words impaled on a file, to be used as evidence against him if necessary. So keep those words short, accurate and pointed.

If you find that a letter is too long, take out your equivalent of the sub-editor's blue pencil. Slash out the surplusage. Rip away the unnecessary wordage. Tear off the extra words with which your thoughts are clothed and leave them to stand on their own merits. If, when naked, you are ashamed of them . . . if your thoughts are embarrassing when stripped of their cover . . . then think again. Redraft . . . rewrite . . . rethink . . . .

Prolixity and excess verbiage not only offend, bore and muddle the reader but fool the writer as well. So be brief, won't you?

13

The Choice of Words – and Words to the Wise

Businesses succeed or fail according to someone's choice of personnel. Two of the best ways of assessing the calibre of a man are through his choice of friends and of books. An author or a speaker makes his impact through the words he uses and the way he uses them. Writers of letters are authors and writers. 'No matter how humble, there's no place like home', sighed the sentimental singer of years gone by. And however humble the letter, there's no place like paper for the use of the apt word or the choice phrase, properly selected.

Consider, first, how one attitude of man may be described in many ways, some approving, some definitely not. Suppose that your correspondent refuses to budge from the attitude he takes. He may be described as stubborn or stiff-necked, mulish, pig-headed, intractable, obdurate, hardline or intransigent, fanatical or thick. Clearly, you disapprove of his behaviour.

But precisely the same attitude on his part may be called: dogged, pertinacious, determined, resolute, steady, constant, reliable . . . In that case, the person is courageous. His word can be trusted . . . someone who will not bend before every blast, or trim his sails to the strongest wind (splendid clichés those – see Chapter 15).

So, adjectives must be handled with particular care. Meaning may be fragile and shatter if struck by the wrong expression.

But the right word (or, to use the more appropriate French expression, the *mot juste* – the word which will do justice to the occasion and which is just right) may be a difficult task. 'I just can't put my finger on the expression I want. What was the word for that? Oh, never mind', says the letterwriter, using whatever expression he can think of at the time.

'What else was he to do?', you say. Well, he could ask someone else to pin down the word for him. Or he could consult that great work: *The Thesaurus of English Words and Phrases* by Peter Roget. Here are collected tens of thousands of words, sorted into categories, with synonyms and antonyms, verbs and adjectives, nouns, pronouns – the lot. It costs little and is available in hard cover or paperback. Every writer and speaker of any sort should have one available.

As no alternative but as a companion essential, you need a dictionary. It makes no difference whether 'you' are managing director or trainee manager. If letter-writing comes within your sphere, you need a collection of words and their meanings. At best, I recommend *The Shorter Oxford English Dictionary* – a witty title when you try to lift its two enormous volumes.

For everyday use, you might try something really short – but a man's intelligence and intellectual capacities tend (correctly) to be judged by the extent of his vocabulary and the precision with which he uses it. So if you do not know the meaning of a word or are doubtful as to its exact import, then look it up.

Only a snob looks down on the illiterate – but the lettered man (especially the one who writes letters as part of his living) is inviting derision and laughter if he mishandles words. If he is a foreigner then, of course, he has every excuse to do so (see Chapter 31 – which includes some horrible examples). But for the man whose native tongue is English, it is vital that when his letters provoke laughter, they should do so by intention and not by mistake . . . when they produce anger, that this was their object . . . that the words used convey the meaning intended.

Language is nothing more than communication between human beings. To communicate accurately the meaning and intent of the writer is the object of the letter. Words are his weapons. They should be selected with the greatest care that the writer's time, education and intellect will permit.

14

Clarity

Parliamentary draughtsmen pride themselves on their clarity of expression. They are trained and experienced in using words so as to give the clearest of meanings. They spend months in the drafting and preparation of bills; then Parliamentarians spend more months in considering the draughtsman's words and altering or amending them; eventually, the Queen signifies her assent and a new law is born.

Considering the toil and travail which went into the pre-natal stages of an Act of Parliament, it is surprising how often the result is so utterly incomprehensible. Lawyers and judges spend a good part of their lives seeking to interpret the words used by the draughtsmen and Parliamentarians. They thought they knew what they meant – but because words so often bear different meanings, the result can be chaotic. Pity, then, the average commercial letterwriter, who cannot spare time for the drafting of his missives. Naturally, draughtsmen and lawyers use precedents. Those in the companion volumes to this should provide a similar prop for the businessman. But still, even precedents must be adapted. And words which may be quite adequate for one situation may need careful alteration for another.

Suppose that you write to a prospective employee that you will provide him with a house. Is he entitled to be dissatisfied with a flat or a bungalow? What a pity that you did not use the words 'residence' or 'living accommodation' or 'home'.

Your assistant has a restraint clause (see Chapter 63) in his contract of service? You do not describe with sufficient clarity the nature of the business which he is forbidden to follow when he leaves you? Then the entire clause may be 'too vague to be enforceable'.

You provide management services? You promise to send in four men to do a particular job? Are you justified in sending women instead? There is a specific Interpretation Act, designed to help in the 'construction' of statutes. 'Man', as Churchill once put it, 'embraces woman'. But does he in your deal? And, anyway, are you in breach of those anti-sex discrimination laws that normally ban 'discriminatory' practices in employment and in advertising?

You can probably find much better examples from your own disputes. Careful, precise use of the English language may take time in the short run but will eventually pay. But clarity is not only concerned with the words you use. It also matters not to begrudge sufficient words to include all the terms in the contract, all the items you wish to cover. Doubt destroys clarity and accurate wording eliminates doubt.

Suppose, for instance, that you include no restraint clause at all in your contract of service. Then do not expect your employee to be restrained from competing against you after he departs. You fix a time for the doing of a job but do not say that time of completion is an essential element of the deal? Then if he is late, you may be powerless.

If you arrange for a builder to do work on your property but do not fix a price, the court will imply a term into your deal that you must pay a reasonable price. 'Obviously', a judge would say, 'the parties must have intended that the contractor be paid for his efforts . . . . The inclusion of this clause was essential in order to give the contract business efficacy.' In general, if the parties have not seen fit to provide for a situation, the courts will decline to do so for them. It is up to you to make your deals, not for the judges to do so.

Or suppose that you launch into freelance journalism. You agree to provide a feature for a trade paper. Then you should say: 'If the article is returned to me within four weeks, then I shall accept it back without question. But if you keep it longer, it becomes yours.' This prevents any later argument about the piece being sent 'on spec', except to the limited extent indicated.

The clearer your own thoughts, the better you will put them down on paper. The greater the clarity with which you write, the more likely it is that your writing will bring the results you seek. Unless you are deliberately trying to kick up dust so as to obscure some unpleasant issue, remember: unless your words are clear, they will not produce the desired effect.

15

Clichés

Good business demands modern merchandising. The presentation of a product matters greatly. Poor, primitive or commonplace packaging or publicity may mean death to a product. Good merchandise may be wasted on the market thanks to unimaginative, old fashioned, commonplace presentation. 'Trite', you say. 'You preach to the converted.'

'Trite, maybe', I answer. 'But you have yourself answered with a cliché – which proves my point. The very same businessmen who accept that merchandising material, packaging and presentation must be original, striking, vital and vivacious are still prepared to package their thoughts in words so well chewed that they nauseate.'

Your thoughts, like your products, should be presented in bright, original wording. Impossible? Then at least avoid the aggravating cliché which slips so easily off the tongue but itself reveals the lack of thought applied by the writer's mind. 'The worse your case, the louder you should shout it', proclaims the demagogue. Certainly the more unoriginal the thought, the more important its disguise.

Have you ever listened to a really skilled politician keeping his audience spellbound with words, full of sound and fury but signifying nothing? Or what of the salesman with the superlative spiel, wrapping his lines in clouds of glory . . . selling goods like hot cakes, before his audience cools off, ruefully realising that they did not really want the goods at all? The speaker pours his words into the air, where they disappear. But he must use them with care and keep them polished.

How much more so, then, must the writer mind his words and phrases? You want your correspondent to read your letters and to act upon them? They are designed to provoke thought or sales or at least the appropriate and helpful reply? Then do the recipient the courtesy of avoiding the cliché.

Wit and humour help (see Chapter 17). So do quotations (Chapter 13). But ordinary, short, simple, Anglo-Saxon words, selected for the meaning required will do just as well.

Rule 1: Never use a long word where a short one will fill the bill. Verbosity in the letterwriter seldom impresses anyone but himself.

Rule 2: The more impo.tant your message, the fresher the words should appear. In one of Howard Spring's famous tales, he recounts how the young greengrocer made his fortune by spraying water over his produce, every morning. 'Fresh with the morning dew', read his notice. He sold his stock. Your ideas should appear fresh, however stale or rotten they may in fact have to be.

We all have our pet hates in the realms of the cliché. Here are some of mine:

'In this day and age.'

'This ship of state has entered stormy waters.'

'This is a memorable occasion for the company.'

'This is a once only, unrepeatable and absolutely magnificent bargain offer.'

'The buy of the year.'

'We must give of our best.'

'Each and every one of us.'

'We are moving full speed ahead.'

'Finally, and in conclusion.'

'Quite frankly . . . frankly speaking . . . to tell you the truth . . . honestly . . . I'll be frank with you . . . genuinely . . . sincerely speaking . . .' Beware of all of these. They may amount only to a turn of phrase, but they do suggest that the writer is well capable of lying, not telling the truth, avoiding genuineness, sincerity or honesty (as the case may be). The really honest, frank person does not need to hang a notice round his neck, to inform the world of his integrity.

'We have the honour to be . . . . We beg to remain . . . . Too true . . . . Now how about that? . . . Your speedy response will oblige . . . . Our grateful thanks . . . .' Ugh!

Clichés, ancient or modern, are a menace. When next you are bored at a meeting, make your own list. 'Much water will flow under the bridges . . . . Many bridges will be crossed . . . . How time will fly by . . . . My grateful thanks . . . .' Have you ever heard of thanks being ungrateful?

16

Officialese

For years, I corresponded with a company secretary. 'Dear Sir', he invariably began. 'Yours faithfully', his letters ended. They were courteous but curt, polite if peremptory – and slightly overpowering in their aloof dignity. Obviously, I thought, the writer is a tough, remote man, with whom it would be a great mistake to tangle.

A short time ago, I visited the company office. There I met the secretary – elderly, benign, gentle. He used his style of writing to disguise his personality and to keep his problems at bay. As he is an official, his letters reflect the policy of the board and the views of his superiors. Like the excellent and civil servant that he is, he keeps himself – and his personality – well in the background.

Official style, then, may provide a convenient shield. But the official writer should still keep his words as incisive as a sword. His position provides no excuse for the blunting of his meaning by use of that jargon which provides the writer with an escape from thought.

This means that clichés should be avoided (Chapter 15). If a letter is routine, it may still be crisp in its wording, clear in the message it conveys.

The most horrible examples of this sort of officialese are thought to be found in epistles from government departments or local authorities. But there are plenty emanating from bureaucrats of the commercial world. 'Vagueness is often necessary', you say, 'so as to avoid making a decision – or indicating that one has not been made. Alternatively, clarity sometimes means unkindness while vagueness may envelop the unpleasant present with future hope.'

A terrible sentence, that. What does it mean? No one says that you must be tactless or cruel – but it is seldom kind to place the recipient of your letter in a sea of uncertainty, unleashed by a flood of long, boring and mainly meaningless verbiage. Whether you write officially or unofficially, personally or impersonally, brevity and clarity should be the keynote of your letters.

'How do we achieve this worthwhile goal?', you ask. Use the precedents in the companion volumes to this. Then take your own drafts and ruthlessly rid them of every useless word, every ghastly, jargon-ridden sentence. Peel off the layers of excess wordage which clothe your thoughts and the bare bones revealed will tell their own tale – far better. Shake off the padding and your bills for stationery and typing will shrink. A well chosen word at the right time saves at least nine out of season.

A famous poet tells how he goes through his verses to cut out the sibilant sounds. 'Chase away the geese', he says, 'and you have a farmyard that sounds infinitely more attractive.' If the letterwriter scatters the jargon before him and uses simple, Anglo-Saxon English wherever he can, he will achieve better results in less space and hence at a lower price. One page of typing may scarcely be worth saving. But just work out how much saving you would achieve when you multiply that page by the dozen, the hundred or the thousand, as you start to duplicate, to make photocopies, to type from precedents. Jargon may have its place as a cloak for the writer, but it should never be used as a muffler for meaning, or a cushion to choke the living daylights out of the writer's thoughts.

17

Wit and Humour

Puns and word play

The humble pun has a bad name. Call it a play on words and it leaps back into fashion. Describe it as a *jeu de mots* and it is *a là mode* indeed.

In fact, much of the best humour results from deft handling of the language. It is precisely for this reason that jokes in foreign tongues are often so hard to enjoy.

The comedian or humourist in speech has many weapons at his disposal. His art is part visual, part aural. The expression on his face may matter as much as that which he gives to his words. A writer who would be a jester has words alone. On occasion, this is a positive advantage. There are no distractions. You do not depend upon audience reaction for results. There is no mass misery to contend with, no 'house' to be warmed. But still . . . .

Reducing the written word into its categories, a novelist or fiction writer can build up a story over his pages. He can create situations which are comic. Even the non-fiction author has his humourous moments – he may use a joke or a witticism to point a moral or simply to enliven the tale he tells.

Letterwriters have less scope for humour. They have fewer words to play with – so their aim must be more sure. And the pun may prove a weapon not to be despised.

'You may bet your bottom dollar – if you will pardon the expression – that you will get more for your money with us.'

'This new line in pens will make its mark (in both senses of the word).'

'We were thinking of advertising these cut-price lavatories as being for customers who were none too flush – but perish the thought!'

Quick wit? Certainly not. But a break from the usual boring epistles. If the recipient groans at a pun, he may still wish that he had perpetrated it himself.

Irony and sarcasm

Sarcasm, say the sages, is the lowest form of humour. Never mind. It has its moments. But it is designed to hurt. And as there should never be hurt without design, this form of attack should be employed with great care.

Irony, on the other hand, is sarcasm with the sting removed. You place your tongue firmly in your cheek, smile gently and (with luck) produce a chuckle for your reader.

'I know that you are immensely busy and incredibly overworked', you write to a representative who is reputed to have done nothing of late save to sit on his rear axle – or, to be more precise, on that of the company car. 'But do you think that you could possibly spare the time to sell some of our new lines? If so, we should be much obliged. If not, then I trust that you will not think it unreasonable of us if we terminate your appointment. You have, to be precise, just one month more within which to reach your target . . . .' If that does not stir him into extracting his digit, nothing will. It is sarcasm, justified.

Irony is more gentle. For instance:

'No doubt there are many reasons for your poor sales record. And when you say it could be worse, perhaps you are right. But we would require some proof of that proposition. Meanwhile, could you suggest how we can survive the summer?'

Or: 'If the wine was as old as the chicken, or the chicken as fresh as the waitress, we would have enjoyed our lunch. As it is, may we suggest that a revolution below stairs would not be out of place?'

At the expense of others

'Taking the mickey' is a pastime to be enjoyed with care. Even those who tease the most may enjoy least the fun poked at themselves. Not everyone is 'a good sport', when the joke is on him.

A careful distinction must be made, in any event, between the private laugh in a confidential note and precisely the same witticism in a letter which may be seen by others. In the first case, the recipient may join in the laughter at his own expense. In the latter, he may feel humiliated and upset. There is all the difference in the world between engaging in voluntary self-mockery and being locked into the stocks in the centre of the village green . . . between accepting a private 'in joke', and letting the laughter publicly out of the bag. So note well the occasion before you provoke laughter which may turn into tears – or, to be more precise, into ill-will, ill-humour – and lost profits.

The sting in the tail

The chairman called the managing director into his office. A few minutes later, the next senior in line received a summons. Within ten minutes, he was followed by his colleagues, one by one, in order of seniority. Eventually, the most junior of all was left outside, worrying and wondering. Then his turn came. He found his colleagues seated around the boardroom table.

'Mr Jones', said the chairman, gravely. 'I wish to speak to you about my secretary, Miss Brown.'

'Yes?'

'Have you been sleeping with Miss Brown?'

'Oh no, sir. Certainly not.'

'Very well. Then *you* sack her!'

The sting in the tail is the main arrow in the quiver of every professional humourist. He leads you up one trail and when you think that you have reached the end, he changes direction so abruptly that you are left mentally standing – laughing at the twist in the trail.

For the speaker, like the General, surprise is vital. So it is for the writer of stories of suspense, detection or murder. A pity that it is not more used by the letterwriter, who seeks dramatic and immediate effect.

Some surprising examples, not all humourous:

Dear John,
Over the course of the past five years, you have earned my friendship and appreciation by a long series of considerable kindnesses. Today presents a memorable occasion. I have the biggest favour yet to ask of you!

Dear Mr Jones,
I fully appreciate that the defects in the machinery which we sold to you led to some considerable unpleasantness between us, all of which was our fault – or, to be completely accurate, that of this machinery which we imported from France. If you were to tear up this letter, you would have every justification in doing so – particularly as I am about to ask a favour of you. Will you be kind enough to allow us to replace the defective machine, at absolutely no cost to yourselves, with another of a different manufacture, for which we are now the agents? Our good name and goodwill are vital to us and . . . .

Dear Jim,
I am writing to confirm that the time has come for your promised increase in salary. You have done a magnificent job and have earned the congratulations and appreciation of us all. The chairman, in particular, has asked me to say how greatly your services are valued.
However, you may wish to treat this letter as a repudiation of your contract of service. As you know, the company is going through a period of very great financial crisis. So you and I are both being asked to accept a postponement of any increase in our salaries. I have accepted the situation. Will you?
Please would you come and see me? I have found this letter a very difficult one to write – and would be immensely sorry to lose you as a colleague. As you know, we have great confidence in the future of the business. But the present is absolute hell!

There are thousands of variations on this theme of the unexpected. Sometimes, the twist is good for a laugh – sometimes it is an introduction to an unpleasant shock. Sometimes the twist is single and gentle, sometimes the letterwriter's path flips back and forth. But the reader's attention is always riveted to the writer's words. What is coming next?

Assuming that the writer is tactful, this off-beat approach will be appreciated. 'It's a miserable situation, but the man has a sense of humour . . .'; 'He's in a hell of a mess, isn't he? Still, things can't be too bad – at least he hasn't lost his sense of humour . . .'; 'At least life is never boring when you do business with him . . . .' A tribute, every time.

This book is divided into chapters and sections, and they in turn into sentences, phrases and (occasionally) isolated words. If the text ran on from beginning to end without break, the eye would close with boredom. By the time the reader reached the end of the first few pages, he would become a sleeper.

So it is with letters. Divisions are vital and brevity the soul of success (see Chapter 12).

Again, the book must package its ideas in separate compartments – of which humour is only one and surprise a sub-division of that. But such divisions are arbitrary and convenient. They may also be misleading.

Taking the lawyer, for instance. He may be an expert in, say, criminal law. But when he deals with company frauds he must be an expert in company legislation. The man who handles your divorce may specialise in dividing husband from wife. But he must also know how to arrange for the division of their property.

Or, suppose that you are involved in a car crash. The police (and hence the criminal law) may be interested – you or the other driver or both of you may be prosecuted for driving dangerously, or carelessly ignoring a road sign, or disobeying the signals of a police officer on duty. But the civil law may be interested – who is going to claim damages – how much and for what?

So divisions of the law spill one into the other. And so do parts of speech or words of wisdom. Laughter and tears go in partnership, throughout our lives – and often in our letters. The same shock that might provoke a smile in one man may produce anger in another. The speaker must judge his audience and the writer his reader. So because we include 'surprise' under the head of 'humour' does not mean that you should not, on occasion, use precisely the same tactic for a completely different purpose. Example:

Dear John,
This is definitely the end of our business relationship.
Yours sincerely

Similes and Metaphors –
Mixed and Other

Comparisons may be odious, but they provide a useful tool for the letterwriter. Use the words 'like' or 'as' and the odds are that you are employing (to use the technical term) a 'simile'. If these are not apt, they are better omitted. They can be both misleading and offensive. But the striking and suitable simile is well worth using.

Hence:

'Our products are small and comparatively inexpensive – but as essential as jewels in a fine watch.'

'Like jewels in a royal crown . . .'.

'As welcome as the story's ending.'

Metaphors omit the 'like' and the 'as'. For instance:

'We will hit them for six.'

'Out first ball.'

'Centre stump.'

'For a duck.'

'We fell at the first fence.'

'This time, we've backed a winner.'

The vital rule with metaphors is not to mix them. Mix your drinks and you become sick. Mix your metaphors and your letter becomes ridiculous. Some typical, laughable examples:

'If you want to hedge your bets, then try reversing the batting order and your scheme may turn up trumps.'

'Business is a battle-field in which poor players get skittled out, often at the first fence.'

'I'm sorry that we cannot give you more credit, but the banks are at our throat and squeezing us until the pips come out.'

'As the Bishop said to the actress: "It's an ill wind that blows no one any profits, when it comes to reducing demand by putting the handcuffs on embattled industry".'

'In a nutshell, good letters and mixed metaphors are as compatible as chalk and Chinese chopsticks, if you see what I mean.' Well, just about . . .

'The last person we want to employ is a 'Yes-man' – don't you agree?'

Part 3

TACT AND TACTICS

Modesty Matters

Not for nothing do royalty and editors use the word 'we'. By remaining in the first person, the writer retains his personality and avoids the impersonal and soulless approach. But by avoiding the singular, he adds strength to his purpose. Without saying so, he indicates that his views are shared by others . . . . The nation, public opinion, the company, his colleagues – or as the case may be – are all solidly behind him.

There are two alternatives. The first is used a great deal by the French – the word *on* – 'one'. But in English, it exemplifies the pompous and archaic. 'One finds it hard to understand your attitude in this matter . . . .' One does, does one? 'One knows your difficulties, but one must take into account the current shortage of credit . . . .' One must indeed. No, this will not do. 'One' is not pleased to accept your invitation to address the board . . . .' – *you* are!

In the first example, you are expressing a personal feeling, on your own behalf; in the second, you are making clear that your views are your own and the recollection and notes relied upon are those of yourself. In the third, *you* are accepting the invitation.

'We appreciate . . .' would be fine, if writing on behalf of the board. 'We have checked our note of the conversation with you . . .' is plain silly, if you are discussing *your* note of *your* conversation. And 'we shall be pleased to come' is appropriate if you are bringing your wife, but if the acceptance is for yourself alone (assuming that you are not an extremely royal personage), the use of 'we' indicates either visions of grandeur or a split personality, neither of which are likely to be appreciated by your hosts.

There are trades and professions with special usages. A one-man firm of solicitors may style himself, extremely grandly: 'W . . . & Co.' – the company he keeps being a secretary, fresh (in all senses) from school. 'We are in receipt of your letter', he writes. Well, he is entitled to put up a front, so good luck to him.

Equally, if you are replying to a letter received on behalf of the company or firm, it is absolutely right to answer: 'We thank you for your letter dated the 14th . . . '. The thanks is that of the institution you represent and not of yourself personally. But if the letter came in an envelope, addressed to you personally and, possibly, marked, 'Private and Confidential' (for the legal rules, see Chapter 62), then it would almost certainly be right for you to reply: 'I am grateful to you for writing to me . . .'. Or: 'I appreciate the trouble you took in letting me have your views on . . .' Or: 'I received your letter and will pass on your message to the board. . . .'

Where, then, you are being dealt with as an individual and written to on a personal level, by all means stick to the singular. But where you are writing on behalf of the business, the plural is generally more apt, more modest and implies greater strength behind your pen.

What, then, of the contents of the letter? How far is 'I' in a letter to be avoided?

Public speakers must avoid like the plague the immodest, boring, self-satisfied appearance conveyed by smug use of the first person singular. 'I came; I saw; I conquered', said Julius Caesar. But he was a dictator and could get away with it. 'We came; we inspected; we took over' is far more appropriate to the modern business world. If you came on your own . . . saw unaccompanied . . . and can honestly say that you were conquered by the excellence of the hospital received . . . then that would be different. 'I am very grateful to you for making my visit so interesting . . . for sparing me so much of your time . . . for the trust you placed in me . . .' You speak personally and sincerely. You write on your own behalf, to thank the recipient for kindness accorded to you.

You may also wish to poke fun at yourself. It is a great deal safer than getting laughs out of the foibles of others. The inimitable Lord Denning delighted in saying: 'When I used to sit and hear cases on my own, I could be sure that justice was done. Now that I spend my time sitting in the Court of Appeal, as one of a bench of three, the odds against justice being done are two to one.' He could get away with it because he is a man who combines extreme individuality and independence of mind with quiet and kindly courtesy. No one takes his jest seriously – least of all himself.

But the writer who obviously sees himself as sitting either in the throne of God, or at its right hand, is a fool. If you have illusions of grandeur, then you would be extremely wise to keep them to yourself or you may find yourself certified. It is no excuse to say: 'I am covering up for my inferiority complex' – your correspondent may come to the same conclusion as the apocryphal psychiatrist – that you are just inferior.

'False modesty is a bad mistake', you say. 'If you happen to be at or approaching the top of the tree, what's the point in pretending that you are still trying to get a foothold . . . .'

None at all. But then it is not for you to shout aloud that you are great. After all, the higher you climb, the further you may fall. One day, you are bound to come tumbling down, if only into retirement or your grave. No one stays aloft for ever. Remember that – and your perch is likely to remain secure for longer. Provoke jealousy by your words and you invite others to shake the tree – or even to pull it out by the roots. There is no need to go to the Dickensian extreme of saying: 'I am an 'umble man' – no one will believe you. Just write with humility, when you can. Modesty matters.

20

Flattery – and the Great You Are

King Canute was overcome by the waves of false adulation, poured over his head. So it was only a matter of time before he wet his royal feet in the waters of disillusion. This sort of foolishness is just as prevalent amongst commoners as it is in the most elevated and courtly circles. Just as it is the height of stupidity to emphasise 'the great I am' (see Chapter 19), so the letterwriter is foolish if he does not cash in on the recipient's inevitably high regard for himself. 'Love yourself', said Oscar Wilde, 'and you are in for a lifetime of romance.' Business people are as romantic as all others.

The courtiers of Canute were intelligent men. They knew their subject and achieved their object – he did not suspect that he was being served a diet of lies. We all like to think the best of ourselves, so one cannot altogether blame the poor fellow. But the letterwriter who does not make use of this universal human failing does not know his job.

Note, first, that flattery is just as useful when your fight is uphill or when you are faced with an unpleasant opponent as it is when you are dealing with someone whom you genuinely admire. For instance:

I have admired your work for so long that I would hate to fall out with you now . . . .

> You are, if I may say so, a man most respected in this industry. So it really does grieve me to have to say . . . .
>
> I fully appreciate your integrity and good intentions, but . . . .
>
> I cannot believe that a man of your great standing would write as you have done, had he known the facts . . . .
>
> I am sure that a company of the importance of yours would not willingly risk sacrificing its good name for the sake of . . . .

You must not underestimate your opposition. The essence of all sound flattery (such as the above examples) is apparent sincerity. A man tries to believe well of himself, and if you share his admiration for his achievements, you already have a great deal in common. The higher and more powerful the executive, the more likely he is to be surrounded by adulators. Like King Canute, he may lap up the praise in unlimited quantities and believe the lot.

Still, where a man achieves eminence in commerce you may expect him to be sound in judgement. Unless his power has corrupted him, he will be suspicious of the flatterer. Hence, subtlety is essential to success. 'Lay it on too thick' and you would be better to 'lay off' altogether – or you may be told precisely where to get off.

Overdo your flattery and it sounds perilously sarcastic. 'Of course you know best . . . . You are as wise as the Three Kings . . . .Naturally, I would not think of arguing with you . . . .' Disastrous overstatements – and dangerous.

Bearing this golden rule always in mind, here are some useful examples of fine flattery for use and adaptation to some commercial occasions:

> The soundness of your judgement in the past is evidenced by your success in the present. May I suggest that you consider using/stocking our . . . in in future?
>
> We are proud that our goods/services have been associated with the name and prestige of your organisation . . . .
>
> We recognise the great contribution made by your company to . . . . Could this not be enhanced still further by . . . ?
>
> We believe that by combining your great experience and reputation with our . . . , the results will be profitable to both our organisations . . . .
>
> We are, of course, only too pleased to demonstrate our new equipment/ machine/methods/services. But knowing the great experience you already have in this field, you may consider this unnecessary . . . .

Our experience in selling/wholesaling/the field of . . . is only equalled by yours in marketing/selecting/merchandising . . . .

Match our computers/equipment/services to your renowned skill and enterprise and we believe that the results will astonish you . . . .

Of course we appreciate your point of view. Your experience in the field is unrivalled. But have you considered the particular benefits of the equipment which we are offering now . . . ?

It is precisely because your reputation is so excellent that we wish to buy from you . . . but can you not help us a little on prices . . . ?

We appreciate that we must pay for your good name . . . but please, not quite so heavily . . . .

Flattery is modesty put to work. Think about it. Instead of saying, expressly or by implication: 'What a good man am I', you write: 'What a grand person are you . . . '. Your correspondent may think you are tremendous – but he is unlikely to retain that view if he finds out that it is shared by yourself. But whatever you write, unless he happens to be an unhappy depressive, he will have a high regard of himself. Commercial executives are especially like that. So cash in.

Suppose that the object of your letter is to achieve some sort of agreement. Whether you are seeking sales or cancelling orders, hiring or firing, it matters not. You are asking your correspondent to agree with your sentiments or wishes. Whether you achieve agreement depends on all the facts and circumstances and (let us be pleasantly immodest – and employ the first person plural), whether you follow the wise advice we give in this book. But to remove our tongue from our cheek, there is one certainty – if you have a high regard for the character, integrity, sense of justice or humour, intelligence and sensitivity of your correspondent, he will agree with you.

So whatever the nature of your letter, the best possible starting-point is praise. If your flattery is insincere, then make sure that this is not visible. If the praise is undeserved, that will make it no less welcome. If your correspondent is susceptible to self-adulation, then he is no less worthy than 99 per cent of his fellow human beings. We are – and we might as well face the fact – a self-centred lot. We are capable of courage, no doubt, and of putting others first. But here are some more universal propositions:

- The executive is interested in his company or firm – but his livelihood comes first. If he is to be sacked, demoted or pushed on one side, the business can go to hell. He (and his family) must be fed.

- Men at all levels of management are likely to be loyal – but only just so long as it suits them. If you want the secrets of your competitor, then waste no money on professional, industrial spies. Just find out who was last to be fired and invite him out to lunch. He will doubtless confide in you and you will acquire most of the information you require, for the cost of a meal and drinks. Commercial hell hath no fury greater than an employee scorned.
- Your correspondent may one day need you more than you now need him; a hint to that effect might do no harm.
- Cynicism aside, a man must earn his living. Attack him and lower him in the eyes of his superiors and you will hardly affect his own exalted opinion of himself. But you will create insecurity, invite hostility and your letter will probably prove a fiasco – unless, of course, its object is to get rid of him.

Remember, then, that your letter will almost certainly be filed, where it may be inspected by others – or even produced in court (see Chapter 70). But if it is of importance, it will be passed up the line. Example? Raise a sticky problem with your bank manager and you can be fairly certain that it will be passed on to Control, at Head Office.

Suppose that you write to a company secretary, attacking his attitude or behaviour or recollection. On receipt, he may be tempted to set light to your words. But the odds are that he will have to present them to his managing director or board. If you want an enemy, then by all means write accordingly.

A famous man once remarked: 'I can deal with my enemies, but heaven preserve me from my friends'. Surveying his troops before the battle of Waterloo, Wellington is said to have observed: 'I don't know what they'll do to the enemy, but they terrify me!'. You will choose your friends, colleagues and assistants as best you can – but in the selection of your enemies your powers of selectivity should be tried with even greater care. The sign over a mid-Western drug store reads: 'We dispense with care'. Many a true word is spoken by mistake. But if you wish to acquire a hostile opponent, then at least do so by design and not through careless choice of words.

So, rudeness seldom pays (see Chapter 22). The converse applies. Build up your correspondent's self-esteem and you do him a favour. Favours breed.

So here again are some tactful words designed to flatter and to please, and without that appearance of insincerity which is, so often, fatal.

Dear Jim,
Experience has taught me to value your views. It is therefore with great diffidence that I suggest that on this occasion you are wrong . . . .

Dear Bill,
As you know, I rarely question your judgement – but have you considered. . . ?

Dear Mr Brown,
I am extremely grateful for the trouble you took in writing to me. I know how very busy you are and your courtesy is immensely appreciated. I do apologise, therefore, for having to take issue with you on just one or two points.

Dear Mr Jones,
As you know, it is extremely rare for me to take issue with you. I am very much a new boy in this business, and rely greatly upon the advice and guidance of good friends, such as yourself. But . . . .

Dear Sir William,
I do appreciate your letter and I am sorry if I have caused offence where none was intended.
    I am sure that you will appreciate the difficulty of my position. I am not a free agent. I have to follow the instructions of my board . . . .

Dear Roger,
As usual, you are right. But dare I suggest . . . ?

Dear Michael,
It is very rarely that you are wrong. But with great hesitation and after a good deal of research, I have come to the conclusion this time that . . .

Dear Harold,
We are old friends and you know the high regard that I have for you. Our understanding over the years has been built on frankness – and I hope that you will not misunderstand my motives – nor regard this letter in any way as an attack on your judgement or, still less, as a slur on your integrity . . .

Dear Brian,
You are a marvel! I followed your suggestion which achieved precisely the desired results. Thank you very much indeed.
                    Yours sincerely,

Dear Mr Green,
As always, your advice was sound. I followed it – with gratifying results. We are very much obliged to you.
                         Yours sincerely,

Dear Mr Dark,
The arguments you deploy would convince an army. May I suggest just one slight amendment . . . ?

Finally, some flattering words, for use when hiring and firing:

We are delighted that you have agreed to join our board, especially as initially the emoluments are not high. We are confident that your guidance will enable this young company to flourish – and the investment of your time will pay financial dividends, very soon . . . .

Many congratulations on your appointment. We are delighted to have you on the board and are confident that your knowledge and experience will add greatly to the potential of the company . . . .

The fact is that you are too big for the company . . . .

We simply do not have a post worthy of your calibre . . . .

We cannot expect you to wait indefinitely for promotion . . . .

In so many ways, we shall be sorry to lose you . . . .

If you are taking on a man at a salary less than you would wish to pay and are grateful to him for agreeing to invest in the future, along with you, then say so. If you are pleased to have him, then tell him just that. When appointing an executive – or anyone else – you want him to feel that he is appreciated and that he will be a happy member of your team. Then boost his ego accordingly.

If you are dismissing a man for misconduct, then of course you must be careful not to let your kindness get the better of you. If you are not giving proper notice or pay in lieu because you say that your employee has behaved so badly that you are entitled to sack him summarily, then do not put words of commendation into writing or they may be hurled back into your teeth, if eventually you are sued. But otherwise, if only for humanitarian reasons, you should do what you can to assuage the pride of the departing employee.

These principles, then, apply to most commercial fields. Fertilise and irrigate them with kind words about your fellow man and he is likely to return the compliment by thinking well of you – and doing well by you.

Praise Him

Praise and flattery are eternal allies. Praise is the weapon of flattery, flattery the product of praise. In the last chapter, we looked at some forms of commercial flattery. Here are some similar precedents for praise:

> We have now had the opportunity not only to test your new product but to assess its market potential. We congratulate you – you have a winner. We are only worried about price. Could you not make this just a little more competitive? Our Mr Jones will telephone you . . . .

> As you know, it is part of my function to criticise. I have had to write to you on several occasions with complaints. It therefore now gives me added pleasure to be able to express our sincere appreciation for . . .

> We are extremely pleased with the way in which you have reorganised your department. We know that you have put in very long hours over the past few months and have really devoted your energies to the task. The board has asked me to tell you that your work is fully appreciated . . .

> Well done! Your campaign has achieved results far beyond our expectations. We hope that you will be able to keep it up . . . .

> You have set for yourself a remarkable precedent. We shall do all we can to help you to follow it . . . .

> We know how much effort you have put into . . . . We are confident that eventually profit will emerge from it. Meanwhile, the board fully recognises that the disappointing results are in no way due to any lack of vision or effort on your part . . . .

> Do not be down-hearted. We all recognise the excellence of your work and the skill you put into it. We know that perseverance will pay dividends . . . .

> Please would you convey to your . . . our appreciation for his/her/their courtesy/efficiency/kindness/assistance . . . .

> The staff who you have allocated to the maintenance of our . . . are excellent. We would be obliged if they could be left with us . . . .

> Heaven may be praised! At last you have . . . . Well done!

The Art of Rudeness

A 'gentleman' is 'a person who is never unintentionally rude'. Intentional rudeness must be for some sensible purpose and designed to achieve effect. In the theatre, it is taken for granted that the effect must be planned, created and perfected. In correspondence, planning equals preparation, precedent and thought. And the effects which require the maximum of all three generally receive the minimum because of anger or anxiety, hostility, dismay or urgency.

Attack usually produces that satisfying counterblast which relieves the writer's tension. You speak your mind so as to get your anger off your chest. 'I must get it out of my system', you say. Or: 'Let's have it out . . . I am not going to bottle it in . . .'

The metaphors are apt. Just as the penitent improves his soul and relieves his conscience by his frankness in the confessional . . . the unhappy sufferer from insomnia obtains relief from torture by opening his heart and mind on the psychiatrist's couch . . . or your friend feels so very much better by pouring out his troubles into your sympathetic ear . . . so hostility is released through expression. Take it out of your mind and you may release it from your memory. 'I'm a frank person, you say. I don't believe in false pretences. Much better to have it out.' (There we go again.)

All this is doubtless psychologically and physiologically sound. But it spells potential commercial disaster. If you get overheated, cannot keep your cool, are unable to apply a thoughtful, careful mind to unpleasant personal situations, then a moment's misery may turn into permanent disaster, your rude letter may result in loss and litigation, aggravation and upset – an exercise that is profitless, in every sense of that word.

So the first rule about writing rude letters may generally be summed up in one word – don't. If the situation requires straight talking, then arrange to meet the other man – and talk. By the time the meeting is held, the odds are that you will have cooled down and your anger may turn to understanding, your wrath to forbearance, your loss of friends and profits to potential future business . . . and in any event, to the preservation of your good name and of your reputation as a man of dignity and restraint. At worst if you do let fly, then at least your loss of self-possession will not be recorded on paper.

'Sorry', you say. 'We have been patient for long enough. We keep getting impertinent letters, and they require a reply. I cannot allow foul-mouthed rudeness to my staff, without some sort of vigorous response.' Alternatively: 'I am certain that if I let off a real blast of indignation, I will bring them up short. Nothing short of rudeness will make them understand the seriousness of the position. A loud shout now may bring results.' Very well. Then sit back, consider – and draft your words with care.

First, avoid foul language like the plague. You can be far more abusive in carefully considered, common words than in those which boast only four letters. In the army, I found that one, simple, single four-lettered word which has a certain Anglo-Saxon pungency about it if used as a verb, becomes a miserable, meaningless bore when used or adapted as a noun, adjective and verb within the same sentence. A one-word vocabularly is scarcely expressive of anything except the user's lack of education.

So choose good words, with care. Remember the purpose for which they are intended and employ them accordingly. Hone the razor's edge of your displeasure with rasping wit. 'I want to give them something to think about', you announce. Very well. Then first think about what you are going to give them. And I repeat – take care.

The turning of the other cheek may be hard, but commercially it is generally sound. An angry word provokes the like response – unless the recipient is well advised (or maybe a reader of this book – which, I trust, comes to the same). Seriously – the driver who proceeds without due care is liable to be prosecuted, is recognised as a menace, and may well acquire penalty points on his licence, to put his folly into permanently recognisable form. The man who sounds off on paper through lack of self-control endorses his words in permanent form and unless he is very careful indeed will soon regret them.

In case you must be rude, here are some literate examples for your studied consideration, please.

Rebuttal of persistent allegations

Yes, we have received your fifteen letters, containing the same allegations. We replied to the first half-dozen, but no useful purpose would be served by our answering each one. Unlike the wine which you and I used to enjoy together before you saw fit to destroy our friendship, your allegations do not mellow or improve with age. And unlike the meals which we shared, the more your words repeat, the worse the taste they leave in my mouth.

I have long restrained myself from expressing my thoughts. But may we now regard this unpleasant correspondence as at an end?

Riposte to rudeness

Having allowed several days to pass since receiving your impertinent letter, and even in the cool light of the weekend, I still regard your sentiments as quite the most unpleasant that I have seen on paper for a very long time indeed. In the circumstances, unless you see fit to acquire some unaccustomed humility and to apologise, this correspondence – and our business and personal relationships – are all permanently at an end.

(Signed)

Note   The absence of a farewell signature (Yours faithfully) is extremely offensive. Silence may on occasion be golden but it is often a good deal more expressive and useful than words. Hence the best answer to many unpleasant letters is simply to impale them on a file, without reply.

Brevity – the soul of brusqueness

This correspondence is at an end.

Sarcasm – to a (former) friend

Will you oblige me and go to hell? When you arrive, you will certainly find yourself in congenial company. I wish you a safe journey.

Brief end to long friendship

Will we pay you more, you ask? No – a thousand times. But not again in writing. My regard for you is no longer worth even a postage stamp.

So we'll sue

Maybe when you come before a court you will learn courtesy. We propose to provide you with this opportunity as swiftly as possible. Your rudeness is intolerable. This correspondence will now cease. Instead, we have instructed our solicitors to issue proceedings against you forthwith.

Two-letter word

No.

Throwing their words back in their teeth

We append herewith a schedule containing particulars of the speeches, impertinent exclamations and expressions of rudeness which have finally succeeded in destroying, utterly and permanently, our regard for you and our business with you. If you were decent people, we would expect a full apology. As it is, no doubt we shall hear nothing more from you. In one way, that will be a merciful relief.

Insensitivity incarnate

You are undoubtedly the closest approach to a rhinoceros ever to walk on two legs. If my poisoned pen has not yet penetrated your inflexible hide, then there is no hope for you. I can only suggest that a holiday might help – and for the sake of us all, I would recommend a very long one, as far away from us as possible.

If and when you return to town in recognisable human form, do please contact me. I shall be pleased to attempt to re-establish our relationship. And you never know, we might be willing to place further orders with you.

Do take care of yourself. There must be those who would miss you if you drove yourself to a premature grave.

Gloating over misfortune

Having received your letters – none of which, we thought, contained sufficient substance to merit a reply – we were not at all surprised to read of the judgement against you in the High Court last week. A few more like that and no doubt your company will be wound up. In that happy event, would you be kind enough to let us know, so that we may have the pleasure of attending the liquidation proceedings?

Water off a sheep's back

As the PR boys say: 'There is no substitute for wool'. If proof of this were required, your letter would serve admirably. It has no other apparent purpose.

Note Have you noticed? The really effectively rude letters are usually those in which the words are barbed with wit or sarcasm – but which have an outward appearance of charm. But then the most devastating rudeness in speech is generally perpetrated with a sweet smile on the face. To lose your temper is a sign of defeat. To lose it in court is often to lose your case . . . to lose it on paper is always to lose face and forfeit the full effect that your words could otherwise have.

So keep cool, won't you? And address your letters with care, marking the envelopes (where appropriate) 'Personal and Confidential'. Watch out for libel (Chapter 56), rejoice that it is not defamatory to tell a man to his face precisely what you think of him. But when you dictate a letter, your secretary (at least) will know its contents.

23

Rude Retorts – at Leisure

'How I wish I'd thought of that', we all say, half an hour after we made a lame reply to a rude remark. The devastating riposte . . . the unanswerable counter-thrust . . . the really rude retort which none the less has a touch of wit – these so seldom come to mind when you want them.

But replies to rudeness – in kind but with compound interest – are a great deal easier, when the initial attack was made by letter. So now suppose that your other cheek has been turned so often that it is sore . . . that you are determined to lash out at last. Then remember that there can be no general rule as to the best words for the occasion. Everything depends upon the occasion itself. You must match your wit to the words of your opponent. You must parry his thrusts at the point of impact and hit back where it hurts most.

Here are just a few sample suggestions:

> We suggest that the best way for you to appreciate the poverty of your case would be for you to read the words with which you have seen fit to clothe it. We are not referring to the grammatical or typing errors when we say that those words are as incomprehensible as they are discourteous.

> The emptiness of your threats is only equalled by the poverty of your product.

> By resorting to blatant incivility, you have not lowered the level of your case. It started below ground. May we respectfully suggest that you let it rest in peace? If you see fit again to disinter it, we shall have it cremated by our lawyers.

> We are not at all surprised that you have descended to common abuse. A dried pea always rattles loudest.

How kind of you to reveal yourself so admirably on paper. Your charming words are appreciated for what they are – a smoke screen.

We are, of course, sorely tempted to tell you to go straight to hell. But as this is an experience which you will doubtless have already had and enjoyed, no useful purpose would be served thereby. Instead we recommend that you strive desperately for the other place. Were you to change your ways completely, you never know your luck. Meanwhile, we do not intend to allow you to make our business life into a purgatory.

If we were to descend to your level of abuse, our words would acquire the same odour as already attaches to yours. Suffice it, then, to say . . . .

If you manufactured fine sticks and stones, instead of cloth *(or ships, or shoes, or sealing wax . . . as the case may be)* then your words might break our bones. As it is, we suggest that you re-read them. They provide a really excellent mirror, revealing the writer's mind . . . .

Finally, then, here is your guide to replies:

1 Never descend to common abuse (it is too common to be effective);
2 Never lose your cool – in person, this may be difficult; on paper, the heat of the moment can always be allowed to pass – there is no excuse for breaking this rule;
3 Bland discourtesy is best – the rude retort, hidden in the sting of an apparently polite remark;
4 There is no better way to annoy your opponent than to laugh at him; apparently gentle words may have far greater effect than any vulgar obscenity;
5 If attacked by a thug, then you get back into a corner and bring up your knee into the man's groin – that is where you will hurt him the most. If attacked by a commercial loud-mouth look for his business groin: take aim and fire hard.

There is, of course, one grave disadvantage to launching a written counter-attack. You are not there when your letter is opened, so you cannot observe the effect it has on the enemy. Now, if the employee dealing with the matter is sacked . . . if you hear no more about the claim which they were intending to make upon you . . . or even if in contrast to your quiet, balanced and witty words, the crudity of the attacks of your opponent becomes apparent – then you will probably have won. And if by any chance your opponent is next seen bent double and moaning – perhaps during the course of bankruptcy or winding-up proceedings – then you will know that your blow reached its target.

Meanwhile, here are some final, rude rebuffs:

I appreciate, Mr Jones, that you are Chairman of the company and cannot possibly spare enough time properly to supervise its business to ensure that it keeps its best customers, but it is really a pity that you cannot prevent your subordinates from writing letters such as that now under reply . . . *(this line is best used when you are quite certain that the Chairman has in fact written the letter himself, look at the reference – Chapter 5. With one stroke, you are rude and hurtful, whilst at the same time giving him the opportunity, if he wishes to save face with you.)*

Naturally, I would not dream of criticising your staff. If you wish to allow them to write letters that destroy your connection, then that is your business – or, to be more precise, that was your business . . . .

We are even prepared to put up with such discourtesy, incivility and boorishness, where the product is satisfactory. But the unreliability of your story is only matched by that of your products. We desire no further contact with either. Kindly address any further correspondence which you may be so ill-advised to write, to our lawyers. Alternatively, it may be that if you consult yours, you may cease to be ill-advised – in which case, we shall look forward to receiving an apology from you . . . .

How kind of you to write in such characteristic terms. That which we have always suspected has now become pathetically apparent. Our business with you is at an end.

May we respectfully suggest that you go to hell? Upon arrival, you will at last be surrounded by friends. These will undoubtedly include the mendacious gentleman whom you allege is prepared to testify on your behalf.

24

Tearing off Strips – Plus Warnings and Complaints

The heat of the moment engenders steam – which should not be let off till you have cooled down. If you must explode, then do so orally and resist the temptation to put your feelings into writing. 'Least said, soonest mended' – and least written, least destroyed.

The object of recording your wrath on paper must be (literally) for the record. You may need to prove why you rejected a product or dismissed an employee, for instance. Alternatively, you may prefer to write because you can choose your words with greater care, so that if ever they are used against you, you are less likely to regret them. Or you may wish the recipient to consider your views at his leisure. Finally, the victim of your wrath may be at too great a distance conveniently to attack by any other method.

You must take particular care to match the calmness of your words to the precise nature of the occasion (see also Chapter 25 on turning the other cheek and Chapter 23 on retorts to rudeness). Some useful examples:

> We enclose herewith a schedule, setting out in detail the assurances you have given and broken in recent months. How much longer do you expect us to endure this sort of treatment?

> We have not completely given up hope of an improvement in our treatment at your hands, but we are about to do so.

> Our patience is exhausted. This must be your last chance.

> Please do not ignore this letter as you have seen fit to ignore those of . . . . Next time, we shall not write but take action.

Commercial correspondence is full of dread warnings of dire results. Some are gentle, some cruelly outspoken, some kind, some cruel. Here are some examples, to be threaded appropriately into your admonitory letter:

> We have had to complain many times in the past concerning . . . . If we have cause to repeat our complaints in the future, then inevitably . . . .

We appreciate that this is the first complaint concerning your.... But you must appreciate that this is a matter of grave concern to us. We must warn you that if there is any repetition, then . . . .

I shall not warn you again . . . .

Please accept this warning in place of the action which we would have to take if there were any repetition in the future . . . .

A nod being as good as a wink, would you please ensure . . . .

The partnership between warnings and complaints is by now sadly obvious. Either may be fended off with the appropriate action, or often by apology (see Chapter 27). But the art of complaining is itself worth careful study – and is not always allied to a warning. Anyone can complain. Only those with power can warn effectively. Before you rattle your sabre, you must ensure that your adversary will be suitably impressed. If the sound resembles a pea in an empty gourd, then threats and warnings are out. But you can still complain.

Complaints, then, may sometimes be allied with threats or warnings – but are often quite as effective on their own. Indeed, where a threat would be laughable or provocative, it is in any event better left out.

The complainant's first task is to discover the best ear in which to pour his poison. Do you go straight to the top man, knowing that as a result you will antagonise the junior executive with whom you have dealt? Or do you exercise patience and keep your complaints on a lower level? Do you let off commercial steam to your trade association or Chamber of Commerce, or try your luck with the trade or professional association of the other man? Only experience can tell. Only after thought should you decide.

The complaint itself may be toned up or down, incensed or outraged, in sorrow or in anger. Everything depends upon the results you seek. Here are a few useful lines:

We would be pleased to retain our association with you, but . . . .

We are sure that you personally could have no idea of . . . .

We wish that this were the first time that we had cause to complain about . . . .

We are very anxious to avoid embroiling the board in . . . , but . . . .

We are sorry to trouble you personally regarding the sins of your subordinates, but . . . .

We have so far restrained ourselves from complaining, but . . . .

We have complained many times. This is the last.

25

The Other Cheek

To turn hostility into a friendship or a row into a firm, fat order – these are the marks of the skilful, commercial letterwriter. Call it cynical, if you like, but if through your calculated coolness you can make the other man feel like a worm, then you will avoid acquiring a needless enemy and will exchange enmity for amity – with profit.

Turning the other cheek, then, may require self-control – but if you cannot control yourself, you should not be in charge of others. Once fire has broken out, the use of a fan will only cause the flames to leap higher. But employed in time, it will cool down the entire situation.

Even after the outburst of hostilities, all is not necessarily lost. 'Softly, softly catchee monkee', says the oriental sage. Cool customers are admired . . . hot-heads lose custom.

So think carefully before you fire off any letter like those in the last chapters. Instead, re-read some of the flattering phrases in Chapter 20, and see if you cannot find the inspiration and the words to change your correspondent's wrath into gold.

26

In a Tight Corner

Metaphorically speaking (or writing), in time of trouble we tend to draw our allusions from the worlds of fencing or boxing. A cutting remark . . . a debating thrust . . . out for the count . . . hit below the belt . . . in a tight corner . . . three cheers . . . and so on . . . .

If you are in difficulties, you must choose your words with special care. To emerge unscathed, you have three alternatives. You can throw in the sponge . . . trade blow for blow . . . or duck smartly under your opponent's fist, and skip nimbly away.

For a change, let us take our first example from the speaker's world. (See *Janner's Complete Speechmaker and Compendium of Retellable Tales.*)

You are proposing a toast to the bride and groom. The bride's father is dead. The groom's parents are divorced. What do you do?

You can surrender by making no mention of the parents. This is abject cowardice, and generally regarded as such.

You can neatly duck the situation by a few, carefully chosen sentences: 'The bride's father . . . we wish he were here not only in spirit . . . but he would have been proud and happy today . . . . How pleased we are that our groom's parents are both so well – and here together for the celebration . . .'.

Finally, you can take the bull by the horns (to take an analogy from a sport of another kind). You can start with the sort of comment given above – and then extend it into the appropriate elegy and eulogy. 'Let us face it, ladies and gentlemen – no occasion is completely perfect, no life without its problems. How sad are we that the bride's father is not here . . . but we admire her mother doubly for the fortitude with which she bore her loss and especially for the courageous and splendid way in which she brought up the bride . . . . The extent of her triumph is revealed by the radiance of our bride today.

'We know, too, that our groom's parents sit together with him, united in their joy at his happiness and good fortune. . . .'

Now suppose that you are writing to the family. You cannot attend their celebration. Normally, the less said about difficulties and differences, the better. 'With you in *our* happiness', reads the cable from afar. 'How sad we are that we cannot join you', goes the letter. But where the parties are close to you and you have to write at greater length, the above principles still apply. Hence:

As you know, I was an old friend of your father. I know how delighted he would have been at your choice of bride.

I am writing to you both, although I know that you are now apart – you will, I am sure, be together for the great day. How I wish I could make up a trio. I admire so much the way in which, despite your differences, you have always managed to be so civilised when it came to relationships with your son. You must be proud of him.

There are plenty of equivalent situations in business. The surrender is achieved by an apology (see Chapter 27). The counter-attack is explained in Chapter 23 (on 'Retorts to Rudeness'). And the form of ducking away from trouble, to be adopted in any particular circumstances, will depend upon those circumstances themselves. Here are some useful, opening gambits:

> We fully appreciate the circumstances which have led to the anger and disappointment expressed in your letter. But there is another side to the story and we do hope that you will give it your earnest consideration.

> You are quite right, on the face of it – but . . . .

> I do see your point of view – but am sure that you will give consideration to mine.

> Yes, we made a mistake – but in all good faith. The situation nevertheless remains that . . . .

> We see your viewpoint. Now please do consider ours.

> Your letter sets out your case quite admirably. It is only courteous, then, for us to set out as fully as possible the situation as we see it . . . .

> Thank you so much for your promptness in dealing with our complaint. We appreciate your letter – and your viewpoint. But we hope that, on reflection, you will agree that . . . .

> We see your viewpoint. Now please do consider ours.

> Your letter sets out your case quite admirably. It is only courteous, then, for us to set out as fully as possible the situation as we see it . . . .

> Thank you so much for your promptness in dealing with our complaint. We appreciate your letter – and your viewpoint. But we hope that, on reflection, you will agree that . . . .

> We genuinely feel that your complaint is based on a misunderstanding. We do see that . . . but would urge you to consider . . . .

> Yes, you are right. But . . . .

> No, we do not agree with you. But nevertheless . . . .

Have you noticed that the man who uses words as weapons employs very similar tactics to those of the fencer or boxer? You give way a little, so as to attack a lot. You retreat gently, so as to counter-attack with firmness. You at least pretend to see the other man's viewpoint so that he will be prepared to consider your. Alternatively, you politely disagree – and then show your magnanimity and/or good sense or goodwill by then offering a compromise of giving in on some point, however small.

The French put it well: *'Il faut se reculer pour mieux sauter'* – you must withdraw, the better to leap forward. As with the weapons of war, so with words of forensic skill, written or spoken. You step back so as to throw your opponent off balance (boxing again).

There are occasions, of course, when you have your back to the wall . . . there is no room for retreat . . . all escape routes are cut off . . . then remember the advice given to policemen, in similar but physical circumstances: 'Tuck yourself neatly into the corner and use your fists, your knees, your truncheon . . . . At least if you are in that corner, they will not be able to get a knife in your back . . .' Unless, of course, they knock you unconscious and drag you out.

Try these gambits, when absolutely desperate:

> If you see fit to make these allegations to third parties, we shall have no hesitation in putting the matter in the hands of our solicitors.

> Your threats are as empty as the premise upon which your allegations are based is groundless. Nevertheless, if you wish to take the matter further we must refer you to our solicitors.

> We regard your allegations as both impertinent and groundless. If they are repeated, we shall take such steps as are advised by our lawyers, to protect both our position and our good name.

> If you are so ill-advised as to carry out your threats, then kindly direct all future correspondence to our solicitors.

> In one, last, desperate attempt to remedy a situation which (we repeat) is not of our making, our Mr Jones will contact you and try to arrange some convenient time to visit your office.

> Our chairman will be in touch with yours.

In the last resort, then, you have three alternatives. First, you can pass your correspondence to your lawyers – possibly in the hope that if you put on a sufficiently bold legal front, your enemies will stay in their own trenches. You can cast aside pride or convention and try the personal approach – at whatever level seems best. Or you can remain completely silent.

An aged employee used to keep a little, wooden sign, hanging on the wall by her desk: 'Silence is golden', it read. On occasion – indeed, on more occasions than most people realise – the adage is a good one. One way to emerge unscathed from a tight corner is to go into a clinch

. . . to cover your face with your arms . . . to crouch low, cling to the ropes and pray for the sound of the bell.

27

Apologies

The most valuable five-letter word in the English language is 'sorry'. If you are liable to lose your shirt, try donning a white sheet. The effect on your adversaries can be quite startling. When a man gets what he wants . . . when his pride is satisfied by the humbling of his opponent . . . when he is king of the castle . . . then he is willing to forgive a very great deal. So every skilled letterwriter must know how to wield a dignified apology.

But in the commercial world, even apologies must be driven home with due care. Where – expressly or by implication – you have admitted fault or liability, on paper, you will be in trouble if you afterwards try to change your mind.

If you are involved in a road traffic accident, for instance, in which there is damage to person or property, an admission of liability may rob you of your insurance cover. Insurers do not wish to lose the chance to fight a case, if they see fit, through some premature genuflection on the part of the insured.

Or take the common case of the supplier or contractor, concerned to preserve the goodwill of the complaining customer. The customer writes, moaning mightily. Instead of replying with a firm denial of liability and contradiction of the customer's allegations, the anxious supplier or contractor simply replies: 'I'm terribly sorry . . . we greatly regret . . . we shall do everything possible to put things right . . .' But the customer cannot be satisfied. He refuses to pay his bill. The supplier or contractor sues.

'Look at the correspondence', retorts the debtor. 'We put all our complaints into writing. They were never denied. Quite on the contrary, the plaintiffs apologised and expressed their regrets. It's a pretty weak excuse to say that they only did this to preserve our goodwill, isn't it?' Weak or not, it is one that is commonly heard in courts.

So take care before you assuage the customer or client who takes umbrage, by apologising in writing. If you feel that the best position from your viewpoint is prostrate, then arrange an interview. Any apology in writing is much more likely to be used in evidence against you.

That said, the art of graceful apology is still worth a careful study. Here are some common and helpful forms of apology, to be incorporated into your letters, when you find it necessary and advisable to do penance on paper.

> Despite our every effort, these errors occurred – and we do apologise. We trust that no substantial or lasting harm was done and we are pleased to have the opportunity to put things right.

> We apologise most sincerely for any apparent discourtesy. None was intended.

> We greatly regret that you were offended by . . . .

> While we are extremely sorry that you felt that . . . , we must nevertheless point out that . . .

> We are always anxious to have satisfied customers and therefore we are prepared to assist by . . . . We are in any event sorry that you were dissatisfied but we must point out that in making this offer, we do so without prejudice to our contention that . . . and no liability whatsoever is admitted. *(For the rules on 'without prejudice', see Chapter 71.)*

> I am asked by our board to say how much it is regretted that . . . . The Directors trust that you will accept their assurance that . . . .

> We apologise most sincerely for . . . .

28

Lies – Black and White

'Let's face it, Judge', said the witness. 'Do you always tell the truth? Even to your wife?' Laughter in court.

'Happily', His Lordship replied, 'I am not here to answer your questions . . .' Happily indeed one tells the truth, the whole truth and nothing but the truth all the time, every time and throughout. Anyway, some lies are forgivable. The letterwriter needs to know how best to disguise the truth.

Sometimes, the truth is just too horrible to tell. Imagine starting a letter: 'I finally decided to skip our lunch because I could not bear the thought of spending an hour in your company.' *Or:* 'The reason why our chairman refused to speak to you is that he regards you as an unmitigated crook.' *Much better to say:* 'Terribly sorry, but I must ask you to be kind enough to postpone our lunch – the chairman has decided to descend upon us that very day, alas!' *Or:* 'I do hope that you were not offended by any apparent discourtesy on the chairman's part. Certainly none was intended – I fear that in the crowd he simply did not recognise you.'

These of course, are examples of the white lie, designed to avoid offence. When the truth would hurt or humiliate, even the moralist forgives the untruth.

What, then of the inexcusable whopper – the blatant lie, told for one's own good only? Just as courts of law are not courts of morals and justice is sometimes cruel, so a book on the letterwriter's craft is no place for moral homilies or preacher's cant. But if lies must be told, at least tell them well – and I suggest the following ten commandments for the purpose:

1   Check all previous correspondence and documents, to ensure that the truth is not apparent from your own previous writings.
2   Comb through your own recollection – and check with that of your colleagues – to ensure that nothing has already been said to your correspondents which would now nail you as a liar.
3   If you can avoid putting the untruth on to paper, then do so – the telephone is a useful instrument for the purpose, but remember that there may be a machine or a shorthandwriter at the other end of the line recording your words.
4   If you do decide to use the telephone as an instrument of untruth, then *you* have the conversation taped, if you can – after all, one lie is bad enough but to compound it with a contradictory untruth next time is unforgivable. A record of your words will prevent this.
5   If you must record your lie on paper, then cash in on the ambiguities of the English language and try to make your words as vague as possible and capable preferably of at least two interpretations.

6   Prepare an escape route in case of need; maybe the transposition of a comma would alter the meaning back to the truth, so that you could then say: 'I do apologise for the misunderstanding, which was entirely due to a clerical error'.

7   If found out and there is no apparent excuse, be prepared to write: 'Although the letter went out under my reference, it was in fact written by my former assistant, Mr Jones, during my absence – I would like to emphasise the word "former". As a result of this episode, he has been dismissed.'

8   It is always better to have your untruthful letters signed by someone else, even in your name. Thus: 'You will observe that the signature at the foot is in my name but not my writing. This was an inexcusable liberty taken by my then assistant, Mr Jones. He has been dismissed as a result. Thank you for drawing this matter to our attention.' (The fact that there never was a Mr Jones is irrelevant.)

9   When you receive a letter containing a lie, remember the above stratagems – they may be used against you; and study Chapter 23 for suitable ripostes.

10 Where the lie is a large one, you have two alternatives: you may either build up to it by a series of minor fibs, or you can shout the big fib from the start, in capital letters. Thus: 'I fear that you could not properly have read my previous letters to you, which state quite clearly that . . .' Or: 'I had not wanted to tell you, but it is necessary now to make a completely clean breast of it. The fact is that . . .' (The fact, of course, is fiction.)

Remember the eleventh commandment and keep it wholly. *Be not caught.*

You may, of course, take this chapter with as many pinches of salt as suits your literary palate. But like it or not, the lying letter is as much a fact of business life as the lying witness is a regular occupant of the witness-box. It may take a thief to catch a thief but you do not need to be a liar to recognise one. Still, to appreciate the tricks of his trade, it is a great help to know them. So if it makes you feel better, re-read this chapter from that viewpoint only. And now look at replies to lies.

29

Replies to Lies

Call a man a liar and you make an enemy. Suggest that he is mistaken and he may well agree. If you receive a letter containing untruths – however plainly stated – pause and look, before you leap into retaliation in kind. Self-restraint often pays dividends.

There are many ways of turning aside an untruth from the other man. A touch of sophistry is definitely justified. Churchill (who was forbidden by the rules of parliamentary debate to denounce a colleague as a liar) referred to an untruth as 'a terminological inexactitude'. A lie by any other name . . .

Here are some suggested ripostes to the lying letter:

I fear that whoever gave you the information upon which your letter is based is himself in error. *(The height of tact, this – your correspondent saves face from the start and is given every opportunity to withdraw without humiliation – an essential in commercial warfare as in all other.)*

I am sure that it is no fault of yours, but clearly your conclusions are founded on a misunderstanding of the facts.

I am most anxious that there should be no misunderstandings between us. If you would be kind enough to refer to our letter of . . . you will see that the facts are not quite as you have stated.

I fear that our recollections of our conversation do not accord. I am quite sure that we agreed that . . . . I have confirmed this with our Mr Jones, who was present. *(What a pity that you did not confirm it to the other man in writing. Or maybe you did. Or if your letter is in response to one from him which purports to confirm the conversation but gets it wrong, then one up to you for actually reading his letter before you filed it. Beware of so-called letters of confirmation which are in fact travesties of the truth.)*

I am sorry, John, but you are wrong. We have known each other long enough to speak frankly, without ill-will or rancour. I am sure that the cause of the trouble was the report of . . . . I know that under no circumstances would you have written as you did, had you appreciated that . . . . I fear that Mr Green must have led you astray.

All my fault, I am sure – obviously I have not made myself clear.

As I am sure your letter was not intended to be offensive, I shall reply in full . . . .

I wish I had followed your suggestion and got everything into writing – as it is, your letter suggests that unless we can get things cleared up fairly fast, we shall get involved in misunderstandings which neither of us wants. Why don't we meet for lunch?

I am sorry, but I simply cannot accept the allegations contained in your letter. These are founded on an obvious misunderstanding of the situation. Perhaps it would help if I outlined our views, in full.

These gambits are handy whether or not your correspondent has in fact been rude or offensive to you. After all, he may have told an untruth or misstated the situation with a smile on his pen (to mix our metaphors – see Chapter 18). But there are times when rudeness is too blatant to be ignored. This does not mean that you should reply in kind. Here are some suggested, gentle retorts:

We have done business together for many years and I still hope that we shall do so in the future – to our mutual advantage. In the circumstances, I shall not reply to your letter in like tone.

We have known each other for a long time and I really am shocked at the way in which you have seen fit to write. I think that someone is stirring the pot. The statements you make are quite untrue – but I am sure that these have arisen out of pure misunderstanding – probably created by someone who hopes to drive us apart. Let us keep cool. I would be happy to meet you.

Surely it does not help the situation to write as you have done? In the circumstances, I shall resist the temptation to answer in like terms. It is a great pity that we are at loggerheads. This is, I am convinced, quite unnecessary.

If I do not answer your rude letter with an even ruder one, I hope that you will not take this as a sign of weakness. Equally, it will not help if I were to indicate my views as to the distortions of fact which turn your letter into second-rate fiction. I would prefer that we try to revert to where we were before this correspondence started, in the hope that we can clear up the mess without the entire matter landing in the hands of lawyers. If we are no longer to do business together, so be it. But at least let us be civilised. It may help if I set out the facts as I see them.

You may have noticed that in this sort of reply the cliché comes in handy. The set phrase helps conceal the unsettled temper. 'You are in error . . . you are mistaken . . . we regret that you are misinformed . . .' – all phrases much better than 'you are wrong', and almost invariably infinitely preferable to 'you are a damned liar' – even if that is precisely what he is. As every merchandiser and PR man knows, both a product and its presentation need careful wrapping up. The noble art of the skilful wrap-up should form part of every course on commerce – with special reference to the reply to rudeness.

30

On a Personal Note

In general, personal notes should be written by hand. This is far more troublesome and time-consuming than dictating to a typist – which is precisely why the handwritten note is so appreciated. Whether you are sending congratulations or commiserations, apologies or thanks, three lines written are better than three pages typed.

If you really cannot spare the time to write (literally), then at least make sure that you 'top and tail'. Have the body of the letter typed, if you must, but you write in: 'Dear Joe . . .' and 'Yours sincerely, Martin . . .'. Or at least add a handwritten PS.

Naturally, it is helpful if your writing can be read. Pity the poor examiners who have to make sense out of the swift scrawl of the schoolchild or student – but there, too, the examinee loses marks because his words could not be read. If you are taking time to write, then at least spare the extra few moments to do so without the apparent haste which the erratic line and the smudged sentence so clearly indicate.

If you want a good reason for careful writing (courtesy apart), then remember that there are those who specialise in reading character from script. This may, of course, be a good reason for having your letters typed – but it also explains why many prospective employers, when advertising for staff, say: 'Please send full details in your own handwriting'.

The object of a personal note, then, is to convey personal thoughts. The more impersonal the form of the note (through being typed or – much worse – duplicated), the less its effect. Conversely, any personal touches are welcome. The method of writing matters – but so also does method of delivery.

For details of normal postal arrangements, please see Appendix 1.

But do remember that if you can manage to send your missive by hand, marking the envelope accordingly, you are setting a special seal of importance and thought upon the contents. If the recipient sees that you have taken trouble, then he will take note.

A note should generally be a separate document, however short. But there are times when it can be added to something else. If, for instance, you have to send a printed circular to a friend, then add a note at the bottom in your own handwriting. Or perhaps invitations are going out for a company party. These have to be printed. Then add three words at the bottom: 'Do come! – Johnny'. Or try: 'Looking forward to seeing you'.

Or you may want the recipient to come to the meeting? Then add a note: '*Please* be there – I need you!'. Or: 'A full turn-out is vital – I know you are terribly busy, but I would be immensely grateful if you could come.'

Impersonal notes are ideal fodder for the fire or waste basket. The more personal the note you strike, the more likely you are to achieve harmony and success. So be personal, won't you?

31

Letters Overseas –
Customers and their Customs

The traditional caricature of an Englishman is not only a bowler-hatted gentleman who sits silently in a train in Britain talking to no one because of his deep desire to preserve his privacy, but also a phlegmatic figure who sits silently abroad, unless and until he finds a foreigner who is prepared to speak English. In fact, this gentleman will soon have followed the dodo into extinction. Nowadays, the Englishman abroad will 'have a go' at the foreign language, even at the risk of making a fool of himself. He knows that if he wishes to make friends and influence business in his direction, he must make the necessary effort.

Take the American, invading world markets. He will arrange crash courses not only in the foreign languages needed but covering the customs of the customer's country. He knows that customers have customs and that these are to be respected.

Curiously, these rules which are almost self-evident in courteous commercial conduct on the personal level tend to be disregarded when the businessman puts pen to paper or (more likely) mouth to microphone.

Peruse almost any file of correspondence with a foreigner. The letters will be filled with jargon which is scarcely comprehensible even to the writer's compatriots and must be quite inexplicable even to the well educated, overseas reader, equipped with his equivalent of 'O' Level English. However fatal jargon may be on the home market (and it may do grave damage even there – see Chapter 31), it may cause the overseas customer or client to throw up his hands in despair and to throw the letter out in disgust.

You may, of course, point with some justified agony at, for instance, the painfully correct and cliché-ridden letters you receive from Germany. With verbs correctly placed at the end of enormous sentences and the writer remaining, as always, a man who has the honour to be your most obedient and respectful servant, you may say: 'Well, they haven't done so badly, have they?' Well, immodesty suggests that they might do even better if they followed my rules. And not all German businesses are a success. Anyway, if you want to do business with them, you must use your letters to best effect, even if they fail to do likewise.

So what are the answers? There are two possibilities only. Either write your letters in the foreign language concerned or else use the English language in a manner least alarming to the foreigner.

Unless you are yourself expert in the nuances of the foreign tongue in question, my advice is – use it for convivial speech or table talk but not for business letters (except, perhaps, for friendly, non-commercial postscripts). There are enough misunderstandings in international affairs without your adding to them by mangling the foreign tongue on paper. By all means flatter and please the foreigner by conversing with him in his own language – but when you get down to brass tacks, you may find that your deal is punctured through your failure to follow the shades of meaning in your customer's language.

Schoolboy French is all very well for a little *amour* . . . the pride of the Frenchman (his *amour propre* if you like) may be satisfied if you address him in French . . . but unless you are a French scholar, stick to English in the letters you write or you are almost begging for misunderstandings.

You could, of course, employ an interpreter or have your letters translated. To supply a translation – or to write (through your interpreter) in the foreign language in question, could do good – but only if the writer or translator is really bi-lingual. If he cannot cope with the shades of meaning in the foreign language, that is bad enough – but it is even worse to employ a person who is a distinguished exponent of the foreign tongue but quite incapable of understanding the English words which you wish to have translated.

In court, witnesses who do not speak English are entitled to make use of interpreters. But even those who make a living out of court interpreting often make a hash of the job. Assuming that they actually translate the words of the witness (an assumption not always justified by the facts), their failure to assess the shades of meaning between one language and another may result in darkness being cast upon the entire situation.

But then it is rare to be truly bi-lingual. And some of the difficulties involved are obvious even when you consider the idiomatic differences in the use of words as between peoples who ostensibly all speak English. I once saw the end of an American romance when I assured my New York girl friend that I would 'knock her up at six'. Differences between lifts and elevators, braces and suspenders, pavements and sidewalks – all should be known. And in the USA, rubbers are worn on the feet.

Or take pronunciation. The overseas lecturer who explained how the invading forces landed on the beaches and created peace for the inhabitants caused chaos by his charming pronunciation of the words 'beaches' and 'peace'. Letterwriters may at least rejoice that foreign words on paper do not have to be pronounced. But spelling may prove crucial. And whilst the spoken word is transitory, once you have committed yourself in writing, the law is unlikely to say: 'That's not what you meant . . . '

So unless you are very expert in the foreign language concerned, my advice is: stick to English or else pay your foreign customers or clients (or, for that matter, your suppliers) the compliment of having your words translated. But send the original English version as well as the translation, just in case the efficiency of the translator is later under attack.

When you do write in English, all the rules in, for instance, Chapters 10 and 11 apply – but doublefold. Stick to Anglo-Saxon, where you can; the simpler the language the less likely it is that the recipient will misunderstand; the shorter the sentences and the clearer the thoughts, the better the business you are likely to do.

Like all rules, these have their exceptions. If you are trying to delay, then selective sentences of specially contrived jargon may send the foreign correspondent scuttling for his dictionary or (better still) off to join the queue at the local translators. He may even write back to seek elucidation.

If you doubt these suggestions, let me add one more – just consider how much pleasanter and more profitable your dealings with your overseas correspondents would be if they treated you as you are advised to treat them. Not for nothing did the Tower of Babel collapse. Some sensible goodwill . . . some simple phrases . . . some trained translators – these might have kept the building erect to this day. As it is, its ruins should serve as a horrible example to all those who treat foreigners on paper without the consideration they deserve.

32

The Human Races

Dear Jim,
I am happy to give you the benefit of my well considered bias . . . .

The recipient of your letter may be as prejudiced as yourself. But he may not be so ready to recognise his defects. Alternatively, you may be dealing with a man who is genuinely of open and intelligent mind. So even if you are tempted to salt your letters with racialist remarks, restrain yourself.

Take a Scot or an Irishman, for instance. He may delight in making jokes about wee women and whisky or brogue and the Blarney Stone (as the case may be) – but this does not mean that he will like them to come from others. The best raconteurs of the anti-Semitic story are the Jews – who feel entitled to laugh at their own miseries and who recognise that it is probably their laughter, as much as any other quality, that has enabled them to survive. But no Jew appreciates an anti-Semitic joke coming from a non-Jew – even if the teller happens to be a close friend.

Nor should you think that the dropping of bricks is the prerogative of the public speaker or private conversationalist. When you write: 'I can assure you that we are working like niggers on your order', how do you know that the man who deals with it is not himself as black as a beautiful, starless night? 'We would not dream of Jewing you', you say, in answer to a query on the price. Your correspondent may have changed his name from Cohen or Levy . . . he may appear as an Aryan . . . but he may remain both Jewish and proud of it.

Jokes about popes, pills and priests may go down splendidly in a white Anglo-Saxon, Protestant golf club, whose clientele is drawn from the ancient establishment. But even a hint of anti-Catholic prejudice in a letter may spell ruin. 'We would never Welsh on you.' 'Like an Arab market place.' 'Eeny, meeny, miny, mo' – all should be expunged. A reference to Eskimo Nell may be well received, but the popularity of the Harlot of Jerusalem is far from universal.

Quite apart from sordid, commercial motives, no civilised man wishes to cause unnecessary offence (for the correct use of rudeness, please see Chapter 22). Even if you do not agree with the customs of your fellow man, at least accord him respect. There is an ancient, rabbinic saying: 'Respect goes before the Law' – respect, that is, for the ways, feelings, attitudes and ideas of others is even more important than adhering to the letter of the law – an aphorism worth applying to all letters, legal and other.

33

Follow-up

The matador hopes to kill his quarry with the first thrust of his sword. If he succeeds, he may be awarded the one ear, both ears, and (most exceptionally) the tail as well. The letterwriter may make a killing at the first shot – so earning himself profit, an appointment, a prize . . . or whatever other happy result the writer seeks. But a follow-up may be vital.

You will find many examples of follow-up letters in my other books of drafts, including letters to debtors and reminders of many kinds. We shall not repeat them here. But the following list of memory-joggers may be helpful – and adaptable to whatever occasion you have in mind.

I did appreciate the time you gave to me. Could you spare, please, just a little more to answer my letters?

At the risk of becoming a bore, may I please remind you. . . .

I do know how very busy you are, and I would therefore doubly value a reply to . . . .

I do not seem to have received a reply to my letter of the . . . I am quite sure that this is due to an oversight on your part. But your early attention would be greatly appreciated.

I would not dream of pressing you were it not that I am myself under pressure.

I fear that unless you can kindly make your decision shortly, I shall most reluctantly be forced to . . . .

I know that I have written to you before concerning . . . I hope you will not mind my doing so once again.

I refer to my letters of the . . . , the . . . , the . . . and the . . . . Could I now please have the courtesy of a reply?

I fear that unless I receive a reply to my letters within seven days, I shall have to . . . .

I am sure that you intend no discourtesy by ignoring my letters – but on reflection you will agree I hope that it is extremely aggravating.

You cut the cloth of your reminder to suit its purpose. But where your first effort fails, do not be afraid to try again. In fact, the more trying you become, the more likely – in some cases at least – you are to succeed.

34

Introductions and References

The greatest favour that you can do to most men is to provide them with the right sort of introduction. Laugh if you like at 'the old school tie'. Deride college friendships. Call it 'the Old Boy network', if you will. But it exists. 'What matters to the good advocate is not to know his law', said the wise old practitioner, 'but to know his judges'. In every field, it is *whom* rather than *what* you know that matters.

But letters of introduction and of reference require special care. If they are inaccurate or negligent, you could be in trouble. If a reference is defamatory, then you could always rely upon the defence of 'qualified privilege' – but if 'malice' is alleged against you, it could be a long, hard fight.

For the law on references, please see Chapter 56. My companion volumes to this book contain numerous draft samples. These should be used with care.

As for introductions and testimonials, the best are the briefest. Brevity is the soul of sincerity. An excess of superlatives destroys the effect. I would suggest the following:

> *To whom it may concern*
>
> I am pleased to recommend Mr James Blank, who has been employed as a . . . in my department for . . . years. I have found him reliable, diligent, cheerful and helpful. I am very sorry that he is leaving me.

Alternatively:

> I would be much obliged for any assistance you could give to Mr William Brown, who has supplied this company with . . . over the course . . . years. We have now moved into a different line of production and can no longer make use of his products. However, we are happy to recommend him and them to you.

Or:

> I am pleased to provide a reference for Mr William Jones. He is a man of energy, tact and initiative who is leaving us because we have been obliged to close down his department. We cannot offer him the prospects of promotion which he deserves. If you require any further information, please do not hesitate to contact me personally.

Finally, remember to disclaim, loud and clear, in all appropriate cases. If a reference or testimonial is given carelessly and causes damage to the recipient, it will be no answer for you to say that you were not paid for providing it (see Chapter 56).

Examples of this are:

> Whilst we are pleased to assist by providing references/information/ advice, these are given on the strict understanding that no legal liability of any sort is accepted in respect thereof, by the company, its servants or agents.

The above reference/testimonial is given without legal responsibility.

No responsibility can be accepted in respect of the above reference/testimonial, howsoever arising.

'*If we accept your claim for allowances, we owe you £30.*'

Part 4

LETTERS FOR OCCASIONS

Letters that Sell

Whatever your business, you must sell. Whether you are a manufacturer, a wholesaler or a retailer . . . a stockist of services – your own or those of your employees . . . whatever your trade, industry or profession . . . the moment that you cease to sell, your business starts to die.

There are goods or services that sell themselves – happy is the man who can simply sit back and live off them. But the vast majority of the bread upon which we live has to be earned through selling.

Some sales may be made by speech. The larger the item, the more profitable it becomes to devote personal time to seeing the potential customer, face to face. The customer may be bearded in his individual den or addressed as part of an audience. Then, direct sales may be made through advertisements – not the province of this book – or by direct mail – to which Chapter 50 is wholly devoted.

But a vast number of the best sales are won through the right letters arriving on the customer's desk, and lost because those letters are off the mark.

Now, there is no such special creature as the sales letter. Nearly every precedent in my companion precedent books and nearly every letter referred to in this book is selling something. Maybe it is goods or services . . . maybe it is your case for an overdraft or an indulgence . . . maybe it is simply your good name or goodwill.

It follows that if you want to achieve a direct or indirect sale through the mail, all the normal rules set out in this book apply to your letter. For instance, you must pay proper attention to the envelopes (Chapter 46) and stationery (Chapter 45); to the presentation of the contents and in particular to the methods of reproduction (Part 6). Your message must be concise (Chapter 12) – 'Brevity is the soul of sales', as one top merchandising man puts it. You must consider ways of signing on and off (Chapter 2) and pay careful heed to opening and closing with a punch (Chapter 1). You use flattery (Chapter 20), humour (Chapter 17) – and sound and sensible modern grammar (Chapters 10 and 11).

There are some special problems. After careful study of your market and bearing in mind the limitations of letter-writing, what is your best approach to the sales of your particular goods or services?

If you have your prospect sitting across the lunch table, if you have found him at his desk, if you are chatting him up in your shop or showroom, or at your stand at a trade fair, then if one approach fails, you can always try another. You can see the effect that your words are having and adapt your style or approach accordingly. You can argue, cajole, pit your wit against that of your prospect. Naturally, you try hard to avoid the wrong initial approach or the making of later mistakes. But because the man (literally) stares you in the face, you are often given a second chance when the first proves unrewarding.

In that case, in the hope of a direct sale, you devote your own precious time. Unless the customer or the goods or services you are selling, or both, are important it would not be worth your time. The beauty of a letter is that it can be sent so comparatively cheaply. But in return you must watch your words with even greater care than if you were speaking. If your notes fall flat, you will get no encore.

Curiously, many of the top selling organisations who work out a careful routine for their sales staff prepare none for their sales letters. Men are taught what to say and how to say it . . . how to react to each reaction of their customers . . . the precise approach to each stage of the selling process . . . they learn how to insert their feet in the doors of commerce and then how to keep them there.

All this makes good sales sense. Why, then, do the very same businesses become so sloppy when they take to the mail for sales? After all, it is much easier to provide drafts for letters than precedents for speeches. And reproduction on paper is far more certain than in either speech or procreation. If you are prepared to devote enough time and thought to your sales letters, you still cannot guarantee that they will 'click' every time – but they should give birth to far better results than you get at the moment.

What, then should you include in your sales literature? Is yours a case for the soft sell or do you plunge right in and hit your customer hard – and preferably below the belt? Do you make a special, introductory offer – or is yours a 'once only' effort? Do you lay emphasis on price or quality, past achievements or future prospects, should you adopt a style that is formal or colloquial?

Precisely because of the infinite variety of circumstances, products and services, of sellers and buyers, of needs and impulses, no one can possibly answer these questions for you. But you must answer them for yourself.

So sales letters require thought and preparation above all else. You should not 'bash out' a letter, 'tear off' a memorandum to a customer, 'dictate a quick "mailing shot" ' – and then have it completed and polished by some subordinate or maybe signed in your absence. These letters count. They must be prepared and written with care. They must suit your purpose or they will not help to achieve it. Apply the rules in this book to the letters you use for selling and you should reap a profitable harvest. But you ignore them at the peril of your livelihood.

36

Applying for Posts – and Selling Yourself

Call it a job, a position, a post, a situation . . . it is still your bread and butter. Apart from your marriage contract and possibly that for the purchase of your home, your current contract of service is the most important in your life.

Contracts of service may be oral or written – and when written they are legal documents and hence dealt with at length (and with precedents) in my companion books to this one. And because these contracts are normally contained in letters from the company, firm or individual employer, letters of appointment also find their proper place in this book under 'The Law on Letters'.

As a preliminary to any legal arrangement . . . as an opener of the contractual door . . . as a means of getting a foot inside the boardroom, the office, the factory or any other place of work – the letter of application is crucial. But of all the letters that the (actual or potential) top man in business has to write, the job application is the most difficult. He is selling himself by direct mail . . . or at least using the mail to invite an offer for his services . . . so consider the best way to perform this immodest task.

First, what made you write in the first place? The answer provides a simple, brief, effective and invariable opening gambit.

I am replying to your advertisement in today's Gazette . . .

I understand from our mutual friend, James Brown, that you have a vacancy for the position of . . .

I have been referred to you by . . .

The chairman, managing director, company secretary, personnel director – the potential employer or his representative – will not at this stage toss your letter into the basket. The door to success is unlatched. Then apply your shoulder:

I am most interested in the possibilities which your position offers.

I appreciate the responsibilities which the successful applicant would bear and I find these exciting.

The challenge offered by your post is one that I would welcome.

Members of Parliament, of local authorities and of the boards of directors of companies all share a duty – they must 'declare their interest' in matters under discussion. If, for instance, you have a financial interest in a contract which your board is considering, then you must say so – loud and clear. If you wish to obtain a place on that board and are applying from the outside, then the more interested you appear in the work that is offered, the more likely you are to get it. Employers seek enthusiasm.

So you have explained the origin of your application and of your interest in the work. You have introduced the subject. Now introduce yourself:

I am 35 years of age, and have been employed in responsible positions in the industry, ever since I completed my Doctorate in . . . at . . . University.

I am at present . . . director of . . . Ltd. You will appreciate, therefore, how vital it is that my application to you be treated in confidence, whatever its outcome.

I have immense experience on every side of the trade. I worked my way up to my present position of . . . from the very bottom.

I am 29 years of age, happily married and have three children. My working experience has been varied. The last eight years have been spent as . . . .

If there are disadvantages in your background, then even these may be turned to account.

Although I have no practical experience of the . . . industry, the many years I have spent in . . . and . . . have provided me with a knowledge of potential markets which I hope you would find valuable.

I started work immediately I left school. Happily, evening classes enabled me to acquire the necessary academic background. But essentially my experience has been obtained in the practical field. It stretches over seventeen years and into every aspect of the business.

Note that the approach is positive. You do not start with an apology: 'I regret that I have no academic qualifications . . . a minimum of practical experience . . . no knowledge of your particular trade . . .' This is fatal. There are rare products that are sold so softly that the 'spiel' begins in an apologetic tone. But these are very rare indeed and do not include yourself. By all means show both honesty and an appreciation of your difficulties by including your demerits. It shows commendable modesty. And this is a great asset when selling yourself. Every really good job appplication combines the maximum of self-praise with the minimum of immodesty.

Avoid the following:

If I am to be accused of immodesty, then so be it. I must tell you that I am highly qualified for the job.

I do not wish to appear immodest but . . . .

Modesty forbids me to set out at length the full scope of my experience.

I do not wish to indulge in self-praise, but . . .

False modesty is insincere. Apparent insincerity is death to the job hunter. After all, if he cannot even put himself tactfully across how can he manage other men or sell a product or organise a business? So away with the pretences. Tell the truth about yourself, with quiet confidence.

Unfortunately, it may be difficult to get the situation you want. You may have to write many letters. So can you take a short cut by attaching to the letter a summary of your life's work and qualifications?

No one likes to buy rejects – unless, of course, he gets them very cheaply. Everyone, on the other hand, likes to think that a product is custom-made for him. The man who buys what he believes that others are queuing up to acquire – but who gets in first, so that he beats the market – is a contented and satisfied purchaser.

Selling your house or your business? Then obviously you would not wish it to appear to be a drag on the market. Lines which 'stick' are sold off cheaply in sales. Conversely, the best way to encourage a customer to buy is to indicate that the goods are in short supply. The retailer who puts a 'sold' sticker on an article is almost sure to get enquiries: 'Can you get one of these for me? Have you any more of these in stock?' One bright spark disposed of a line of real stickers by putting a large sign on the counter which read: 'Sorry – only one per customer . . . .'

So your application must not appear shop-soiled. You do not wish to be an apparent reject.

The rejection slip is the lot of every journalist. But if a piece is panned by one editor, there are always others. Still, he will not write to the second, third or subsequent editor saying: 'This piece has been rejected by . . . and . . . . Would you like it?' If he is wise, he will either have the piece (or at least the top sheet) re-typed.

The higher the position you seek, the more important it is that you appear to be 'just the man'. While you are asking for the post, you must quietly indicate that the job is crying out to be done by you. The salesman shouts: 'Last few only . . . hurry and buy before stocks run out . . . . I can offer you a special, unrepeatable rate . . .' The customer feels privileged, contented, eager to buy. That is the feeling that your letter must instil in your potential employer.

So by all means include a *curriculum vitae* – separate from but attached to your letter. But make sure that parts of it are in the letter itself (as in examples already given) – and that you introduce it with care. Thus:

> To avoid overloading this letter with details, I am taking the liberty of enclosing an account of my background and experience.

> I hope that the enclosed curriculum vitae will be helpful.

> I have prepared for you a brief account of my experience, background and personal details, which I enclose herewith.

Under no circumstances should the 'enclosed details prepared for you' be duplicated. The extent of your lie becomes emphatically apparent. (Please do not laugh – I have seen this sort of incredible error perpetrated dozens of times by job applicants who remain applicants always.) Personalise even the documents that are sent out to all and sundry. Re-angle them, re-type them, remodel the words, the introduction, the ending. Above all, be selective in the facts that you present.

Selectivity is the keynote to successful self sales. Study your market. Read the advertisement. Find out what the company does. Put yourself in the shoes of the selectors. Ask yourself: 'If I were them, what details would I want? And which would I regard as unnecessary? What facts would impress, which would depress? What should I include and what would be tactful to leave out?'

It is not always possible to know the precise work for which you are applying or even the exact nature of the business which advertises for staff. But before you write, you should at least get some general idea.

I used to select staff for an organisation which includes in its name the word 'Bridge'. It has nothing whatsoever to do with card games, but every batch of applications contained at least one in which the writer praised his own skill as a card player. He brought a touch of hilarity to the selection board, but never got an interview. If he could be that careless, we would not waste our time in seeing him. Our advertisement was clearly worded, so his interpretation of it showed lack of care or of intelligence or of both – and either disqualified him for an executive position. And even if he had been in doubt, he should have had the good sense to prevaricate his answer or to check by telephoning *before he committed himself to paper*.

Now, there is a phrase which has become so commonly used as to lose its true meaning. A pity, because it expresses its meaning quite admirably. When you put your application on to paper, you commit yourself. And just as courts will not commit a man for trial on a serious offence without careful consideration, if you want a trial you should not commit yourself on paper without deep and quiet thought.

When you come up for interview, you are almost certain to be asked why you want the job. Work out the answer before you apply for that interview or you may never get one. Ask what they want of you and see how you can best indicate that you can fulfil their needs. You are writing a sales letter, but you have supreme difficulty because your product is yourself. How extraordinary it is that the same man who will spend many, useful, thoughtful hours, drafting his letters for products or services will not spare five minutes when it comes to disposing of his entire working time.

37

Interviews for Jobs

An interview is basically a one-sided negotiation which, both sides initially hope, may lead to a concluded contract of service. There are no laws concerning the carrying out of that interview, but its outcome should always be confirmed by letter. With luck, both sides will be satisfied. The prospective employer will offer a contract of service – and the prospective employee will accept that offer. In any event, courtesy requires that the employer inform the interviewee of the decision taken – or, if the interviewee does not want the job, then he should write and say so.

If the employer has offered payment of expenses, then by coming to the interview the interviewee accepts that offer – and those expenses must be paid. Otherwise, the law does not require that the prospective employer pay one penny towards the interviewee's fares or meals – even if he has had to travel from Land's End to John-o'-Groats and back again. This is peculiarly unfair because the interviewee cannot deduct those expenses, for tax purposes – they are preliminary to the obtaining of work and not incurred (wholly or necessarily) in the course of his employment, even if the interview bears good fruit. The company (or other interviewer) on the other hand, may deduct such expenses, if paid out.

Invitation to be interviewed

Dear Mr Brown,
We shall be pleased to interview you for the post advertised. Would you please call at the company's above address and see our personnel manager, Mr Jones, at 12.15 p.m. on Monday 18 July. If this time is impossible for you, would you kindly telephone Mr Jones and arrange another mutually convenient appointment.

I confirm that we shall be pleased to pay your fares and other reasonable expenses involved in attending the interview.

Appointment offered

Dear Mr Smith,
Thank you for attending for interview. I am instructed that your

application for the post has proved successful. I shall write to you in detail within the next few days.

With kind regards,

Application refused

Dear Mr Brown,
I regret that it has not been possible to offer you the post for which you kindly applied. We were deluged by applicants, many of whom had a great deal more experience in the field than yourself. May we nevertheless thank you for your application and wish you every good fortune in the future.

Applicant rejects offer

Dear Mr Green,
Thank you very much for offering me the post of . . . . After anxious consideration, I have decided not to change positions at the moment.

Applicant rejects, again

Dear Mr Grey,
My company has made me an offer which I find irresistible. In the circumstances, I have decided to stay on in my present post – and, whilst thanking you for your kind offer and for the time which you gave me, I must decline to accept the position with your company.

38

Retirement and Thereafter

Retirement may mean exile to some seaside town or sheltered village, for senior citizens. But most men are put out to grass when their appetite for work is undiminished and their desire for rest is small as their need for money is great. So they leave one position to hunt for another.

Many of the letters in Chapter 36 can do yeoman service, irrespective of the user's age. But here are some suggested, additional sentences:

I am retired, but not retiring – I have twenty years' experience of merchandising and I wish to continue to put it to good use.

My company operates a compulsory early retirement scheme, so as to make way for the young. For this reason, and this reason alone, I am now seeking alternative employment. My interest in my work and my ability to carry it out are equally undimished.

I am in far too good health to give up working – and I have several new schemes for improved production/improved data processing/personnel selection/which I am itching to try out.

Since my compulsory retirement three months ago, I have had the opportunity to undertake refresher courses in computer programming, management methods and general business administration. These, combined with my forty years of active experience in the industry, make me anxious to begin my new career without delay. I would be happy to call upon you.

I am as physically fit as I am mentally restless, and I want work.

My younger colleagues and I worked in complete harmony. It was a rule that the company made inflexible in order to provide incentive and opportunities for them which has resulted in my being forced into early retirement. Your company, I understand, is more concerned with mental agility and with physical energy and commercial experience than with a man's age.

My years of experience being great, I trust that my years of age will not disqualify me from the post you offer. My expectation of active working life is at least ten years. By then, I hope to have made a thoroughly firm and useful impact on your . . . department.

It is true that I shall bring with me years of age – but at the same time, I have an accumulation of knowledge and know-how, skills and experience which are probably unique in the industry. These have been acquired, as you know, in the service of . . . Ltd. Due to their compulsory retirement scheme, they have no further apparent use for my talents. I would greatly appreciate the opportunity of talking to you, and of indicating some of the respects in which I would hope to be of long-term service.

Please would you see me? I have some extremely interesting information which I would like to discuss with you. I am desperately upset at having been forced into early retirement – but the knowledge and know-how, skills and contacts acquired in the service of my former company will, I believe, be of great potential use to you.

Your letters, then, must indicate active virility, youthful energy – plus great experience, culled over the years. The very defects of age which have caused your dismissal may prove the greatest assets to your re-employment. Avoid the miserable old phrases: 'I am a youthful 65', or 'I am an active, middle-aged person'. Be positive in your approach.

Are you applying for a position at a much lower salary than you were previously enjoying? Then do not say: 'My needs are now much smaller. I am prepared to accept less than I previously got.' The former allegation is probably untrue and the latter is all too obvious. Anyway, why should you not start climbing the ladder, once again? Many of the world's greatest mean achieved their eminence long after companies retire their executives. De Gaulle, Churchill, Adenauer, Eisenhower . . . the list is legion.

39

To the Press

Letters to the Press are the Briton's safety valve. But however much the writing of such a letter may improve your humour, merely to receive a curt note of acknowledgement from the editor and then fruitlessly to scan the letters page for weeks thereafter will probably put you back in the same miserable frame of mind which the exercise began. If you want your letters to be published, follow these simple rules:

1   Be concise. In spite of all the rubbish that gets into print, the extraordinary fact is that nearly every paper (trade and commercial, local and national) is short of space. A rambling epistle ends up on the spike.

2   Avoid defamation (see Chapter 56). Of course, if you are writing 'fair comment on a matter of public interest', all will be well. You are entitled to comment – that is, to express your opinion. But any facts upon which the opinion is based must be substantially correct. The opinion need not be 'fair' in the sense that it is reasonable or sensible – the most outrageous views are entitled to

(and often get) an airing on the letters page. But it must not simply be a disguise for a malicious attack.

Most editors are anxious to keep out of trouble with the laws of libel. The smaller the paper, the less likely the editor is to be 'fearless'. But a famous Sunday national rejected (and paid for) a commissioned article from a writer on the ground that, albeit accurate, it might cause offence to people with whom they were anxious to keep on friendly terms. When I gently suggested that they were meant to be '*the* fearless paper', the then features editor replied: 'We must have a paper to be fearless in!'

3 The swifter your reaction to the news . . . the more topical your piece . . . the more cogent your reasoning . . . and, of course, the more highly respected and well known your name or that of your organisation . . . the better your chances of getting published. The letter itself then makes news.

One further suggestion. It is often worth telephoning the editor or letters page editor of the paper concerned and asking whether a letter on the subject you have in mind would have any reasonable chance of publication. This line of attack is usually useless for the nationals – but often handy for the trade, commercial and specialist media. Nobody will ever guarantee you that your letter will appear but if it is written with the blessing of the top man, at the very least he may feel ill at ease in leaving it out.

As for precedents, the field is so wide open that examples are hardly worth giving. For the paper's opening and closing preferences ('Dear Sir', perhaps as opposed to 'Dear Editor', or perhaps, 'Dear John' – and 'Yours, etc.' as opposed to 'Yours sincerely', etc), see the column. As in all other aspects of business, if you want to sell (even for nothing), study your market. Try to fall in with the idiosyncrasies of the paper.

This is not to say, of course, that you are expected to accept the views of the editor. Basically, there are two main sorts of letters arising out of editorial policy – and the paper normally publishes examples of each. The first (well loved, naturally) is in sympathetic praise, and designed to encourage a continuation of the pressure and publicity already given. The other is designed to present the opposite side of the coin and, if possible, to moderate the paper's future effusions on the subject.

To the Editor – attacking editorial

Dear Sir,

My company is deeply involved in the Smoke Town Development Scheme. We regard it as vital for the future of this entire area. With it, adequate and varied employment is almost guaranteed. Without it, the disease of stagnation from which this town has been suffering for a considerable time past is likely to be exacerbated. Youngsters will continue to leave the area in search of better employment. This in its turn will deepen the air of recession and depression which has in the past done much to keep new industry away. And there is little hope for the future.

While appreciating the disadvantages which you have so succinctly explained in your recent editorial, we are frankly surprised that you do not appear to welcome the development as a whole. To find the local newspaper fighting local progress is sad indeed. And we would at least like your readers to know that all criticisms of the development are most carefully considered; that every effort is made to produce schemes which will cause the least possible disturbance and the maximum advantages to the amenities of the neighbourhood; and that (commercial advantages apart) we sincerely believe that when this development is complete, the changes it will bring to the area will prove welcome to all.

Knowing the fair hearing which you give to those whose views differ from your own, I do hope that this letter will be published. We really are anxious that our company's position on this matter shall be known – and that your readers should understand that there is another side to the case which you have so far presented.

Note:

1 Remember that the editor always gets the last word – so vituperation may not only keep your letter out of the column but provoke a reply in kind, which may be more harmful to you than your aggressive approach was to the paper (or to the case which you are seeking to attack);

2 As in all other aspects of life (commercial and private), aggression and hostility tend to provoke the like response. Attacks which are reasonably subtle, as well as being civil and well reasoned, generally produce far better results than the vituperative verbal attack;

3 The above letter would be greatly strengthened if a paragraph could be added, setting out (in brief, concise sentences), some of the facts upon which the writer relies, to show that the development concerned will help the area, and/or that care has been taken in its preparation;

4   For general rules as to opening and closing gambits, the structure
     of the letter itself and the use of words, the usual suggestions
     (contained in this book) apply.

In support of editorial policy

Dear Sir,

It was a pleasure to read the clear and concise explanantion of the aims of
the Smoke Town Development in your editorial last month. May we just
add one further word? We believe that, in the long run, the capital which
will be attracted to this area will benefit not only the industries which will
be represented on the new estate, but everyone in the town. After all, a
revived local economy combined with new and well paid employment will
bring money into the shops, work to those who provide services of all
kinds and satisfaction to the local householders of every category. That,
certainly, is our wish – and that of all others concerned with this project.

Enclosing letter to editor – supporting paper's policy

Dear Mr Smith,

We were delighted to read your editorial in your last month's issue – and
hope that you will find it possible to publish the enclosed letter in support.
Another shoulder to the wheel may do no harm! And – alas – the
development has so many detractors that were it not for your lively and
helpful support, we would by very pessimistic about the future. Thank
you so much, in any event, for your guidance.

We would be very grateful if we could have 2,000 reprints of the
editorial concerned. Is this possible? How much would they cost? If you
could kindly get the appropriate person to telephone our Mr Jones (on
extension 85), this would be much appreciated by us all.

With renewed thanks and hoping to see you again soon, and with all
best wishes for a happy New Year.

Note:

1   A covering letter often helps. If you know the editor, so much the
     better. If not, then it can still do no harm. And even if the letter
     which you want to have published is an attack on editorial policy,
     a covering note can do no harm (see the precedent which
     immediately follows these notes).
2   Give careful thought as to who should sign the letter to the Press
     and that to the editor. In general, the more weighty the name of
     the writer, the more likely it is that his writings will be published.
     If the writer of the covering note is different from that of the

letter, an explanation should be given (again, see next precedent).

3   Remember the service that papers usually provide, willingly and at quite a low price – the provision of reprints. These are often the most helpful, influential and cheapest forms of public relations material. And the papers like them – after all, whilst they are providing publicity for you, you are inevitably returning the compliment.

**Enclosing letter to editor – attacking paper's policy –
from someone acquainted with the editor**

Mr Brown,
I am taking the liberty of sending you herewith a letter from our Chairman, which we all very much hope that you will publish. We appreciate that it contains an attack on your editorial policy – but we know that your shoulders are broad and that you are seldom unhappy when your editorials provoke a lively reaction! We would have preferred, of course, to have written in support of your policy – but know that you will not take it amiss if we hope that your views will not be immutable and that the words of our Chairman may not only influence your readers, but (dare we hope it?) even yourself?

Anyway – and quite seriously – we would all feel much better if the other side of the controversy could be ventilated through the words of our Mr Black.

Meanwhile, my kindest regards – and apologies for troubling you – and with best greetings for the New Year.
Yours sincerely

Note:

1   This letter is suitable for a public relations officer or less senior executive, on friendly terms with the editor. The editor will, of course, realise that the letter signed by the big boss was probably drafted by the PRO or junior executive – but no matter. This approach at two levels often achieves good results.

2   Do not forget to extend the courtesies of the season (even – as in the precedent preceding this – where views differ). The intelligent antagonist makes it clear that there is a distinction between the high regard he has for the editor and his paper as opposed to the poor view that he takes of the opinions under attack.

Enclosing letter to editor – attacking paper's policy – from a stranger

Dear Mr Brown,

I am taking the liberty of enclosing herewith a letter from our Chairman. I do hope that you will manage to publish it – there is extremely strong feeling here that the other side of the picture does need to see the light of day.

I am asked to tell you, also, that if you or any of your staff would care to meet us on site, arrangements would gladly be made. We feel sure that we could provide information and help which would assist you in what we appreciate is a difficult task.

Yours sincerely

Note:

1   Even though the writer does not know the editor, he has taken the trouble of discovering the editor's name. This distinguishes the covering note from the 'Dear Sir' letter intended for the column – and subtly flatters the recipient.

2   Finally, remember that editors are busy people, so the shorter and more pointed your remarks, the more likely they are to reach the desk of the great man himself – rather than that of his deputy assistant. And while a touch of humour is often helpful (as in the last precedent), especially where the writer knows the recipient, it must be handled with even more than usual care, where the parties do not know each other. After all, the editor's sense of humour may not be your own (see Chapter 17).

40

Congratulations and Condolences

Sincerity is the keynote of the good personal letter. Slush is unpleasant for the feet in snowy times and revolting to the mind whatever the occasion. Here are some precedents of the few, appropriate, welcome words that a situation of joy or sorrow requires.

Congratulations

Dear John,
Well done! Myra and I were delighted at your good news. We wish you
every good fortune.

Well done – but formal – on promotion

Dear Mr Jones,
I have been asked by my Board to tell you how very delighted they were to
read of your promotion. They wish you every success.

On honour

Dear Sir William,
Together with all your colleagues in the industry, we rejoice at your new
distinction. We wish you many years of good health in which to enjoy it.

Recovery from illness

Dear George,
We were all delighted to hear that you are back in harness.
Congratulations! We hope that you will now keep fit – and that you will
resist the temptation to overwork. As my wife puts it, in her charming
manner, we businessmen are pretty useless underground, so what's the
good of killing ourselves?
   Please join me for lunch, as soon as possible. Meanwhile, best wishes
from us all.

Condolences

Dear Mrs Smith,
We were shocked to learn the tragic news. Your husband was a
magnificent colleague and a man whose opinion, company and
judgement we all valued. We shall miss him.
   We all feel very helpless – but if there is anything that any of us can do to
be of assistance, we would regard it as a favour if you would not hesitate to
let us know. Meanwhile, my colleagues and I send you our warmest
regards and our most sincere sympathy. We share a deep feeling of loss.

On death of wife

Dear Bill,
What can I say? We were all so very fond of Mary. I know that even
though she had been suffering for so long – and to that extent, her passing
must have been a merciful relief and release for her – it must still have been

agony for you to see her go. We would all like to be of help to you, if we can. Is there anything we can do? Please phone or write or call. We really would like to do something constructive, if possible.

It occurs to me that you might like some help with the legal miseries of winding up the estate or dealing with personal effects. If we can take any of these worries off your hands, please tell us and we will put the company solicitors on the trail. Their probate department is very efficient.

Janet joins me in sending you our fond sympathy. We hope to see you soon.

Note:

The formula for letters of condolence should be:

1 Sympathy.
2 Comfort – which includes words of praise for the deceased.
3 Offer of practical help – if possible, in concrete terms.
4 A touch of normality – including suggestions for future meetings, and even a small touch of humour.
5 Tact – which generally includes the avoidance of emotive words such as 'death'. 'Passing' is a fair substitute. But usually, you need not mention the circumstances giving rise to the letter – they will be only too painfully obvious. Do avoid pomposities like 'sad demise', 'tragic passing on' and 'the world to come'.
6 If you know the survivor to whom you are writing holds strong religious beliefs, then write a letter such as that which follows – but otherwise, the words may be regarded as tactless (at worst) or cant (at best).

The comforts of religion

Dear Mary,

I know that Bob's life was given up to the service of other people – not least through our church. I am sure that the world in which his spirit now lives for ever will be one free of pain, where his good deeds, fine character and remarkable unselfishness will receive their reward.

Meanwhile, Jenny and I send you our most sincere sympathy. We would like to be of help in some way and as we are coming up to town next week, we will take the liberty of telephoning to see if we can drop by for a chat. If we can be of assistance before then, we would be very pleased if you would contact us.

I need hardly say how shocked and upset we are at the news – but we are confident that, with God's help, you will find strength.

Our fondest greetings to you,

Condolence – husband dies

Dear Mrs Smith,

The sad news of your husband's passing was received at Head Office today, and on behalf of the Directors and the Staff I tender our sympathy to you and your family in your loss.

From the time your husband joined our Company, he earned everyone's respect, and we have lost a valued colleague and friend.

As some measure of tangible help at this time, I must inform you that Mr Smith was a participant in our Staff Life Assurance Scheme. In due course, you will receive a cheque for £ . . . from the Trustees of this fund.

Our insurance company will need a copy of the Death Certificate and probate of your husband's will. If Mr Smith left no will then Letters of Administration will be required. Any solicitor will advise you how to apply for these if that course is necessary, but, if there is any help which I or my assistant Mr Brown can give you, then please let me know.

41

Thank You

Call it a 'bread and butter' letter, if you like – but there is none more important. The person who considers that he is entitled to be thanked but who receives no words of gratitude is only equalled in his anger by the man who is thanked inadequately.

Thank you letters need not be long. But they must be sincere and apt. They should preferably be handwritten (see Chapter 30), where they are personal – such as thanking the recipient for hospitality. But on business occasions, they may be incorporated at the start – and probably repeated at the finish – of an ordinary, routine letter.

Here are some thankful openings and closings:

My wife and I are very grateful to you for your hospitality, which we greatly enjoyed – and which we now look forward to returning.

We cannot thank you enough for the way in which you and your wife put yourselves out to make our visit to . . . so happy and memorable.

We did enjoy the hospitality of your home, the company of your family and friends and the theatre evening which you arranged for us. We hope that it will not be long before you and your wife visit . . . . Our home will then be yours – and we hope that you will feel as at home in it as you made us feel in yours.

It was a delightful lunch – which I enjoyed. It was a pleasure to break the business routine in your company and I am grateful to you for your time and hospitality.

Many thanks indeed for your courteous kindness to me when I visited your works.

My Chairman has asked me to say how greatly he appreciated the courtesy extended to him when he visited your factory. He will himself be writing to your Chairman, very shortly.

Your letter was immensely appreciated. Thank you so much.

It is no exaggeration to say that, thanks to you, yesterday was the most memorable day which we have had for a long time.

I cannot resist the opportunity of expressing once again our appreciation for your courtesy and kindness.

We are very grateful to you for your help, which went far beyond the call of duty.

You have done us a very good turn – and we look forward to the chance of repaying this debt of gratitude.

We do appreciate your help – and are grateful for it.

You are a good friend and your assistance was much appreciated.

It is really a delight to work with people who are not only colleagues, but also excellent friends. Thank you for . . . .

It is a pleasure to compete against you! Your courtesy and consideration last night were enormously appreciated.

I hope that you will not feel that our relationship of supplier and customer in any way affects the sincerity of my gratitude to you – quite on the contrary . . . .

Finally, we would like to express once again, our appreciation for . . . .

In conclusion, we send our renewed thanks for . . . .

With our renewed thanks and all best wishes.

Thank you once again for . . . .

Very appreciatively yours.

Next, who better to thank than a grateful customer or client? Thus:

Dear Mr Green,

Your letter dated the . . . has been received by the Managing Director, and he has asked me to write to you to say how grateful he and the other members of the Board are for your kind remarks.

We always make every endeavour possible to ensure the satisfaction of our customers, but it is a source of great pleasure to us all, when we receive letters of appreciation such as the one which you were kind enough to write.

My Directors very much hope that our business relationship with you will continue for many years to our mutual satisfaction.

Your kind sentiments are being conveyed to . . . , and the staff at . . . .

Thank you again,

So far, we have looked at letters of thanks for favours received. But offers may also be acknowledged with gratitude. Refusal may need to be both tactful and graceful. Here are some helpful formulas:

It was extremely good of you to ask me to . . . . I am very upset that I cannot accept.

I have tried hard to put off a previous engagement for exactly the same time as your . . . , but without avail. So I must refuse your invitation – but I do so with tremendous regret – and hope that you might ask me again another day.

My trouble is an overfull diary. I so wish that you had asked me just a few days ago – as it is, I have a prior appointment which I cannot possibly cancel.

How very good of you to invite us! And how very sorry we are to have to decline.

Once again, I fear, duty must come before pleasure. I cannot accept your invitation, because on that very day . . .

As our American friends put it, could I please have a raincheck on your invitation? I simply cannot get away from the office/works/factory/shop at the moment.

I do hope that you will not be offended at yet another refusal. Somehow, our meeting seems to be fated.

It is very kind of you to ask my wife and myself to visit you at home. But we both feel that this time the hospitality should be ours. As it happens, the date you mention is very difficult for us. May we instead suggest that we would welcome a visit from your wife and yourself to us on . . .'

I am always happy to add profit to pleasure. Your suggestion of a business lunch next week is one that I would accept with alacrity, were it not that . . . . As it is, please forgive me – and perhaps our secretaries could fix another day, convenient to us both?

Then what of the guests who do you a favour by coming? There is the lecturer to your Rotary Club – specifically invited by you and possibly giving his time because he is fond of you – or needs your goodwill. Or a colleague works overtime to help you to replan your works. Or maybe your son deserves a pat on the back for some commercial kindness – all too often, we forget that those closest to us are still entitled to our gratitude – and that if they earn it, we are very lucky.

So here are some useful lines of appreciation for services rendered:

You fill your time with service to others – and we are both proud and privileged that you spared your afternoon last week, to visit our . . .

We are extremely grateful to you for speaking to our staff/board/ sales representative/sales conference/management trainees. You will have noticed how attentive they were to your words. But perhaps the greatest tribute of all was the bombardment of questions, which you so kindly took in your stride. It was with great regret that I had to conclude the meeting. We all hope that you will come again. Meanwhile, we are very grateful to you.

No father is entitled to favours from his son – and that I get so many from mine really gives me enormous pleasure. Apart from being an honoured offspring, you are a good friend to your aged dad and I am grateful.

I do really appreciate, Father, the confidence you have placed in me. I am also grateful for the financial security which you have now given me. I shall do my utmost never to let you down.

I would like you to know how grateful I am to you for the help you have given to me in this very difficult period. We are now through the woods – I do not know how I would have survived if it were not for your support.

Finally, a word of thanks may serve as an important reminder. For instance:

Just a note to thank you very much for sparing me so much time during my recent interview. I greatly look forward to hearing from you.

It was very good of you to agree to . . . . We all look forward to your visit on . . . . I confirm the details, which are . . .

Thank you so much for saying that you would send me . . . . This will be immensely helpful.

It was very good of you to promise . . . . Your support/help/action will make all the difference.

42

Appeals

For a letter to be appealing, it must have direct and personal relevance to the reader. The wealthier the recipient – the greater his reputation for generosity – the more letters he will get. Several benevolent millionaires have told me that they receive anything up to two hundred appeal letters in a week. Naturally, most of the 'round robins' are consigned to the basket. The vast bulk of replies must say 'No'. The ones that produce results are almost invariably those from people whom the would-be donor does not feel that he should disappoint.

At best, the ready response results from altruistic benevolence. The cause is worthy and the giver is willing.

Often, self-interest plays its part. The best 'prospect' for the heart foundation is the businessman with cardiac disease. The softest touch for the home for backward children is the father of a mentally retarded son or daughter. The man who gives his ten pounds to the trade benevolent association may wonder whether, one day, he may need its help.

Self-interest takes other forms, too. People like to leave a touch of immortality for themselves or their families through the naming of a building or a bed, or an inscription in a book or on a roll of honour. Honour – approval, popularity, dignity, appreciation – and through them, perhaps, power. The search for these attributes motivates many a generous gift.

Then there is money. Every businessman knows that to earn you must spend. And those who send forth their bread upon the waters of charity may harvest some commercial gratitude. Call it sordid blackmail if you like – but when the chairman of your main customer company asks for a donation for his pet charity, how can you refuse?

Anyway, you have your pet project, haven't you? Doubtless the day will come when you will write to the man who raided your pocket, saying: 'I am sorry to be a nuisance, but the cause is excellent'. He will sigh, reach for his pen and return the compliment which you paid him in the past. He is president or treasurer of his charity, you of yours. The cynic may have little use for either of you. But the organisers of the charity and (far more important) its beneficiaries, will bless you both.

We all want blessings – and need them. Faith, hope and charity are the bastions of our world. The doing of good deeds and the giving of charity lie at the root of every religion – and even those who are irreligious may respond to non-secular appeals, just in case. Well, you never know do you? And anyway, to be cursed is extremely unpleasant.

So the successful appeal-maker has much in common with the salesman. He must study his market and frame and angle his letters accordingly. Each has his own methods. Study those of the successful – and copy them. Before you criticise, consider the results.

A famous *'schnorrer'* – a Jewish beggar by a much kinder and more appreciative name – is said to have approached a leading Rothschild. 'Will you help me?', he asked.

'You know that I do my best not to refuse help', replied the charitable magnate. 'But I really do feel that when you come to see me, you might at least wear clean and respectable clothing.'

The man looked down at his shabby garb and then up at his prospective benefactor. 'Mr Rothschild', he said, gently. 'Do I presume to tell you how to run your bank? No. Then please do not tell me how to beg!'

So learn from others. Make a collection of the appeal letters, brochures and circulars that you receive. Ask yourself: 'Which ones strike home to me? Which have meaning and vitality? Which make me pay?' When you know that, your research is becoming productive.

Usually, you will find that the letters which are really appealing have sincerity, simplicity and personality as their keynotes. And their presentation is sufficiently unusual to remove them from the ruck. And anyway, the ones that really matter will be enclosed with a personal note. Thus:

Dear Bill,
As I expect you know, ever since we discovered that David was mentally

retarded, Mary and I have thrown ourselves into the work of the Happiness Home. Unfortunately, the place is desperately understaffed and cannot cope with half the children who need help. The greatest shortage is cash. Please will you make a donation/join our organisation/take an advertisement in our brochure/*(or as the case may be)?*

We do know the many calls that are made on your generosity – but this one is very close to us. Thank you so much.

Alternatively:

Dear James,
This is my year as chairman of the Trade Benevolent Fund. The need is enormous – as the enclosed pamphlet will show – and the fund does a vast amount of good. I hope that you and I will never need it, but many others do. I am enclosing a circular about ways in which you could help – and I know that you won't let me down, will you?

Many thanks,

Again:

Dear Johnny,
We are desperately broke. We scraped enough for the enclosed brochure and covenant forms. Please would you help? I look forward to hearing from you.

Or:

My dear Sir William,
Forgive this personal approach, but I do know the great interest you take in the Trade Benevolent Fund. If your company would help us this year, we would be immensely grateful. Your last year's contribution was £1,000. As we ran up a £10,000 deficit during the twelve months just ended, we are asking our contributors to be good enough to increase their donations. Would you please help in this way? The Fund really does do magnificent work – but it could not operate without the assistance of the leaders in the trade.

With all best wishes,

PS I have wrung the necks of my own Board, and I am happy to say that my organisation will be giving £5,000 to set the ball rolling.

A few more rules, then:

1   The best fund-raisers are those who give – of themselves and of

their money – they win by example;

2   Ask the recipient of your letter to write back to you personally – so that he does not think that he will get away with it by sending a few miserable pennies to some impersonal appeals organiser;

3   Make things easy, if you like, by enclosing a reply paid envelope – and never forget to send covenant forms, unless you are dealing with a charitable trust – many people are willing to give a larger sum over seven years, if it costs them no more than to give a smaller one right away.

If ever you get really stuck, find someone who is a successful fund-raiser, ply him with some judicious flattery – possibly washed down with food and wine – and he will doubtless help you and not just to draft your letters but to set up your appeals machinery. Nowadays, collecting money for charity is very big business indeed. It is highly competitive and requires the best organisation, if it is to produce even reasonable results.

Finally, a word from the head of a very generous charitable foundation: 'When I receive beautiful brochures on splendid art paper, I get cross and the charity generally gets nothing from me. If it has that sort of money to throw away, then it cannot be as short of funds as it says.'

The converse, from a rival philanthropist: 'You must spend money to raise money. Unless you have a good-looking, well produced and professional set of literature, I will not believe that you are a well and professionally run charitable organisation in which I should invest.'

There must be a happy medium somewhere.

34

Collecting Correspondence

You may, of course, keep your own letters because you dream that one day these will be published. Dreams cost nothing, provided that they do not occupy too much space in your files or time in your day – so good luck. Others one day may recognise the original genius which only you are now sufficiently intelligent to appreciate – but then no one knows you better than yourself.

In general, though, it is a far more profitable occupation to collect the letters of others whose greatness is already known. Bearing in mind that the copyright in the collected correspondence of others rests with the writers (see Chapter 55), the words of the great have considerable value.

There are many dealers in manuscripts and autographs who make an extremely good living through selling the letters of others. You can collect (surprisingly cheaply) the personal and public notes of kings, queens and princes. Prime Ministers' letters are sometimes sold for a song. The more famous the writer and the older and rarer the letter, the higher its cost is likely to be.

Or specialise in literary letters. Many writers and poets of genius were also prolific and distinguished correspondents. There is nothing new about the letterwriter's art. Quite on the contrary. In the days before the telephone and telegraph, the letter was the normal (and often the sole) means of communication.

Remember, too, that letters were written long before the invention of postal services. Roland Hill invented the stamp but not the envelope. You may not be able to buy the original of the epistle to the Corinthians, but you may well discover a note from Napoleon or Nixon, a word from Wordsworth, a letter from Lyndon Johnson or even a scribble by Sir Winston – and if the price is right, buy it. The odds are that it will not only prove a splendid investment but meanwhile look marvellous in a frame.

I know one business man whose lavatory walls are covered from floor to ceiling in the framed and precise wording of the great. Now, there's graffiti for you . . . and what a marvellous way to ensure that both you and your guests may sit at leisure and contemplate your good taste.

It follows, naturally, that if you ever receive a letter from a famous personage, you should keep it. If it comes to the company, you have no right to purloin it – but get permission from the top and this may be permitted. One reason why manuscripts are often marvellously underpriced is that their value is frequently unrecognised – but now, at least, not by you.

Bear these principles in mind before you throw out ancient letters from the loft. There, among the undiscovered Rembrandts, you may find some highly saleable scripts. Far more likely, there may be some ancient stamps on the envelopes. These may not prove as valuable as you had hoped. But a penny saved is nowadays at least tuppence earned, and if you keep the stamp on the cover and the cover on the letter, you may have a dusty goldmine on your hands. Anyway, as I said, a dream is still free and untaxable.

44

Occasions for Letter-writing

It was an occasion of dread boredom. The dinner was bad, the company mediocre and the speeches dragged on towards midnight. Only one person at my table looked engrossed and happy. He was making notes of the speeches on the back of his menu card.

'Quotable material?', I asked him, when the evening eventually reached its morning end.

'That's what you were meant to think', he said. 'Actually, my wife is abroad and I was writing her a letter!'

So I learned my lesson. When I am out speaking in public and someone scribbles at my side, I am not flattered. He is probably writing a letter.

But I have taken a (literal) leaf from that diner's menu card. Agendas and minutes, blank at the back, provide a monstrous temptation to scrawl a note of affection to far-off friends – or even a skeleton draft of a letter, written at leisure and to be dictated and dispatched when time is short:

> Dear . . . , I know that you will forgive the paper upon which this note is written – but at least it will indicate that I really am spending the time when you are away, immersed in miserable business!

> Dear Bill, You will see from the enclosed where I am – I wish I were not! Anyway, there is nothing like a touch of complete after-dinner boredom to provide the incentive for me to drop you a note, to thank you/to remind you/to commiserate . . .

Of course, there are limits to the people who would regard this sort of note as a compliment. The same style and stationery that is ideal for close relations may destroy good relations with those who expect a more dignified approach. As I said, you can always prepare notes for them.

So next time you are sitting on the platform, listening to dull speeches or enduring wretched boredom at any sort of gathering – pick up your trusted pen and the nearest available scrap of clear paper – and write.

'Someone has been messing with the duplicating machine again Miss Lindley?'

Part 5

SUPPLIES, SYSTEMS, STAFF – AND MODERN TECHNIQUES

Stationery and Supplies

Your letterheads, notepaper, compliment slips and stationery are a valuable shop window. If they are scruffy, inartistic or ugly, they will give a bad impression and in the result do you or your business harm. If they are neat, well laid out and handsome, your correspondence is far more likely to have its desired effect – whatever that might be in the particular circumstances.

Why, then, do so many able people devote such little time and thought to their stationery? 'Oh, just order in some ordinary letterheads. Same as last year will do. Leave it up to the printers, they'll produce a design for us. Don't bother with proofs.' Fatal statements, these.

If you want your letters to be telling, then your tale must be typed or written neatly and accurately, on well designed and competently printed paper.

If you are in business, do you spend a fortune on advertising agents, buying space in the Press or on television? Do you take pride in your window display? Then why not spend just a few pounds on getting a professional designer to plan your stationery. You would not begrudge the money if you were preparing a sales leaflet. Well, whatever you write you are selling yourself.

Again, you may spend much money on preparing and registering a trademark. So why will you not spend a little on a design for your stationery?

False economy, then, is more frequently seen in the realm of commerce than in most others. By all means cut the time spent by your staff and yourself on correspondence – the use of good precedents should help. Save through improving your system of work or office administration. But spend just that small amount more on the paper upon which your letters are written, and even in the short run the money should prove very well spent.

These suggestions apply, of course, in every sphere of commercial correspondence. But they have special application when you are writing letters of the law. After all, as a tired toreador is once alleged to have remarked: 'A little bull goes a long way'. If you want credit, to fend off legal proceedings brought by your debtors, then appear prosperous – which is impossible, if you write on paper more suitable for a schoolboy's excercise. You wish to attract top management? Then you must give the impression that you operate a top outfit – so make sure that the design at the top of your paper will advertise your modern and business-like approach.

You would not allow your staff to look slovenly, when dealing with your clients or customers, now would you? Then now is the best possible time for smartening up the stationery upon which they present your written case to the world of business and of the law.

46

The Outside of the Envelope

Every attractive woman knows that appearances count. Every top salesman recognises that first appearances matter most. But the scruffy, disreputable, uninteresting, poorly presented envelopes that first greet the recipients of letters are almost beyond intelligent belief.

'I can't spend a fortune on envelopes of pristine white', you say, trying to justify the miserable brown objects that you send out. Nonsense. The top mail-order companies make sure that even if every letter goes out by the thousand, the recipient feels that he is one in a million – the one that counts; which is reasonable, as he is the one whom it is intended shall pay. (See also Chapter 50, for more on direct mail sales.)

Naturally, there are limits to this doctrine. Nobody feels better about getting a bill if it happens to be in a splendid cover. Accounts should be sent out as cheaply and expeditiously as possible. But letters should be dealt with differently – even if they are requesting payment of accounts. They are part of the front of your business. You should make sure that it is polished.

When dealing with mass mailings, sticky labels can be useful, the products of modern addressing machines. But where your letter is personal, have the envelope neatly typed. Note the form of title for the recipient (Chapter 8 gives details). Check that the name is properly spelt. As for the address it always helps if this is accurately inscribed.

If your letter is intended to be personal to a particular individual, then mark the envelope accordingly. If you do not want the executive's secretary or the director's assistant to read the contents, then mark the envelope: 'Personal and Confidential' or 'Strictly Personal and Private'. Underline the marking in red, if you wish. (For the legal effects of opening employees' mail, please see Chapter 62).

If there is no indication that the contents are no one's business other than that of the person named, then you should not be surprised if anyone else in the business happens to open it and to read it. Great men do not generally sort and sift their own mail. If your letter is intended for the personal attention of the addressee, then the envelope must say so, loud and clear. The contents of the envelope matter – but so does the humble cover itself – far more than most business letterwriters ever realise.

47

On Files

There are several objects to writing a good letter. First, you trust that it will produce the appropriate effect on the recipient (whether that effect be action or inaction). So much for the top copy. But the carbon may be equally important. It will jog your memory, as required, concerning the contents. And it may be used in evidence . . . produced at a hearing, or used in advance to show the strength of your case and so preventing one. Copies matter.

On the other hand, the finest, cleanest copy of the most brilliant of letters is useless if you cannot find it when required. Hence the need for the most effective filing system you can afford.

This book is no place for a discourse on systems for filing. Apart from the general rule that the simpler the system, the more effective it is likely to be, my advice is: spend time, thought and care in creating or adapting a system to suit your own needs. Commercial enterprises which depend enormously upon the accuracy of their records will spend millions upon the development of their products and begrudge a few pounds necessary to establish the appropriate arrangement for their files. Of all business economies, this is the least worthwhile – if only because a really good system will keep the filing itself to the minimum.

Of course, once you have a system, it must be used, intelligently, accurately and well. But how can this be achieved, keeping human error by (probably) overworked and none-too-brilliant juniors to the absolute minimum?

Simplicity, as always, provides the key. At best, each letter will carry the reference number of the file and/or the reference of the matter in question (see Chapter 5). If it carries neither, then the typist should be required to mark at the top right-hand corner of the carbon some identifying number or reference which will make the finding into child's play. If a child cannot operate your filing system, the odds are that now would be an excellent time to change it.

48

Notes

The art of making and using brief notes can save the letterwriter a vast amount of time. If correspondence is written (literally, as well as metaphorically), you can cast your eye back over the lines and amend, re-amend, excise or add, as you see fit. But where you dictate on to a tape, it becomes an aggravation to move back any further than the last sentence or two. Whilst it is much easier for a shorthand typist to flip back through her work on to the passage you require, there is an aggravating and inevitable waste of time while she does so. And if she happens not to be in the first category of readers-back, you may end up by sending her out to type what she has done – and then to hack that around. Notes can avoid much of this misery – and combined with the appropriate precedents can, in many cases, obviate it altogether.

The best system for notes? Jot down the ideas you wish to convey, at random. Then (preferably on a second sheet) put them into logical order. A one-word note should convey a paragraph of dictation. The notes create the skeleton for your letter.

Notes should be brief. There may be some crucial sentence that you need to work out in detail – but if there are many of these, you would be better off to dictate them (still, if you can, in their logical order) and then, if necessary, to re-dictate from the first complete draft.

The first object, then, of a note is to help you to form a clear, concise and accurate letter, incorporating the ideas that you want to convey.

But there is a second purpose. A note jogs the memory. It need not be written at the same time as the letter or even just before. An executive should carry a notebook or diary at all times, and should acquire the art of jotting down ideas as they come to him, otherwise they are bound to go – often never to return. These notes can be incorporated with the later ones, made shortly before the letter itself is written.

In practice, the experienced letterwriter (or, to be more precise, the dictater of correspondence) will find that his need for notes gradually lessens as his experience and skill increases. Once you are used to putting your notes into logical order and dictating them in letter form, you will gradually find that you can sit back and put your thoughts into proper order without committing them to paper. But the more flowing the letter . . . the more polished a man's writing . . . the more precise his wording . . . the less superfluous verbiage . . . the more likely it is that he has mastered the art of using simple notes for complicated thoughts.

Finally, many notes must be taken at meetings or even at business meals, to remind you of arrangements made with some other party. Sometimes, this can be left to an attendant secretary or scribe. But often, the executive must do it for himself – particularly if the meeting concerned is a private or informal one. In that case, you must make a note at the time . . . and accuracy becomes all important . . . and so does concentration upon the business in hand, which you are recording.

How do you achieve precision in note-taking? Ideally, by using shorthand. It is a pity that the art of swift writing tends to be regarded as the preserve of the secretary or professional shorthand writer. It is an enormous asset to any senior manager or executive.

Even the simplest of abbreviations help – know the 'grammalogues' (as they are sometimes called) – that is, the tiny signs, used for the most common words – and you can cut down your writing time by a quarter. Then leave out the vowels and another twenty-five per cent disappears. The words 'and', 'or', 'of', 'but', 'if', 'company' and the like, occupy an inordinate amount of space in ordinary script – to say nothing of the somewhat less common, but equally well used 'public', 'private', 'board', 'director' and so on.

A few hours spared to learn even the most basic forms in shorthand can save, in the course of time, many weeks of hard and unnecessary labour, whilst adding to the accuracy of your performance. Shorthand writing is a rare example of a person being more accurate by working quicker and without any man-made aid other than paper, pen or pencil.

No matter how advanced you may be in your years, there is no reason why you should not start learning simple shorthand. There is no need to enrol into a secretarial course with the youngsters. No doubt the business could afford to provide you with a private teacher, even for an hour or two a week. Indeed, one of the more sensible secretaries on the staff would probably be pleased to teach you half a dozen shorthand abbreviations a week, which you could then practice on the backs of newspapers in the train or, in place of your usual doodles, at boring meetings.

As for the young executive, he should be prepared to train himself in this simple skill, or else the business should make sure that he is taught by others. If you have children, my advice: no matter what their future, make sure that they spend a little time while young in learning to save a great deal of time when they get older. Anyway: more of this skill in the next chapter.

Learning to type is another matter, and one which is a great deal more difficult, time-consuming and, in most cases, unnecessary. Naturally, if you can handle a typewriter and wish to bash out your own correspondence, then well and good. But most executives will leave this side of the business to the secretary or typist. They can avoid it. But note-taking (preferably in shorthand) is a necessary chore, and not necessarily an evil one. A good note has saved the executive many a bad letter.

These suggestions apply throughout every field of professional, as well as commercial, letter-writing. The barrister or solicitor who can take a careful note of a judgement, in shorthand which he is able to read and transcribe, is blessed with a great asset. The architect or surveyor, able to jot down, swiftly and with precision, the requirements of his client, will not only save himself time but will undoubtedly please the client whose precious moments are also spared. Doctors, in any event, use their own form of shorthand for most of their reports.

But if business or professional people have to prepare lengthier documents (which may, for example, be produced in the course of litigation), then to make fuller notes before they finalise these would help them in many ways, and would ensure that they get better results and more satisfied customers or clients than is possible as most of them work at present – at speed, and often leaving out essential information which a few minutes' careful thought and some judicious notes would avoid. Result? Further letters from the solicitors concerned, asking them to fill in the omissions, and extra expense, cost and aggravation all round.

So notes end just before the letter begins. A few moments' pause to reflect on the contents of the letter, pen poised to produce the appropriate notes, can save a vast amount of loose writing, or time-consuming rewriting. The more that your letter matters to you, the more it matters that you should use pre-prepared notes and thoughts in advance.

49

Abbreviations, Shorthand and Letters to Yourself

'What is the world, so full of care, we have no time to stand and stare . . .'. If we have we would prefer to do our standing and staring outside business hours, preferably with our wives and children – otherwise we may lose the former and alienate the latter. So both from his own viewpoint in person and from that of business, the letterwriter should welcome any acceptable short-cut.

Now, writing in longhand is undoubtedly a fantastic time-waster. Hence the shorthand typist and the dictating machine are vital (see Chapter 51). There are some communications with others which must still be written in longhand (see Chapter 30). But letters to yourself should be in shorthand (as discussed in the last chapter).

Consider how many man-hours you spend, over the course of a year, 'jotting down notes', recording conversations or ideas, memoranda, or writing out drafts, to be transcribed at some later date by your secretary. If you could cut your writing time by three-quarters, with no loss of efficiency, you would not only save time but nervous strain.

'Ridiculous', I can see you saying. 'At my age . . . in my position . . . to go off and take a course with little, prospective shorthand typists . . . .'

No need. You can teach yourself all you require in odd moments. Indeed, my unpatented quick shorthand method requires no teaching whatsoever.

First, omit every vowel. Not for nothing did the ancient Hebrews invent a system of writing where the vowels were inserted above and below the letters, in children's writings or where doubt existed – but not otherwise. In fact, the vast majority of vowels are completely unnecessary to understanding.

Next, evolve your own system of abbreviations. Words most commonly used can be replaced by letters or signs. Ten minutes' thought can produce your own list. Here is a sample:

'C' = the company; 'P' = product; 'Pt' = profit; 'L' = London; 'Bd' = board; 'F' = factory; 'S' = shop; 'O' = order.

Take any of your files and work out the words which appear most often. Consider the items which you write out in full which could be abbreviated without difficulty. Create your own shorthand.

Then buy a book on teach yourself shorthand. Ignore the lines and twists, the signs and circles which can help you to build up whole words – long before you have perfected the system, the odds are that you will have retired from the unequal battle. Instead, just learn the quick few symbols for the most common words in the language. In Pitman's method, for instance, they use so-called 'grammalogues' – thus a full stop for 'the', where not attached to another word . . . a tiny circle on the line for 'is' . . . a short, diagonal line for 'of' . . . and so on. The reduction in writing time achieved by using these few signs is great, the time required to learn them very small.

Finally, abbreviate some prefixes and suffixes: '-ion' becomes 'n'; 'super-' becomes 'sr' . . . and so on.

And that is all. You now have a system of shorthand that is quite adequate for most purposes. You have worked it out in a couple of hours and have perfected it in a week. You have saved yourself countless hours of effort that is completely profitless, in both senses of that word.

Naturally, you can afterwards dictate from your notes either to your secretary or to your trusted machine. You may even be able to train your secretary to read your shorthand. Why not? Plenty of secretaries read back each others' notes. Teach your shorthand to your son at college and instead of writing to you once a month, he can write once a week with precisely the same enthusiasm (or lack of it). He can also take down his own notes in the class and lecture, supervision or tutorial, with maximum speed. For this, he will bless you – and blessings from our children are not lightly to be turned aside.

What, then, of the ordinary, humble abbreviation, commonly used in commercial correspondence? In Appendix 2 you will find a list. Do not depise it. Abbreviations are a form of shorthand, accepted in the business world. They save time, effort and paper – provided that they are used accurately and sensibly. Time is the enemy but, unlike most others, needs to be saved if the businessman is to survive unulcerated.

50

Selling by Mail

'Direct mail' means selling through the post. The cost is high – printing, postage, stationery . . . addressing and 'stuffing' envelopes . . . and the building-up, buying or renting of lists of customers or clients. So the letter itself must strike its target with swift and unerring aim or the exercise will be a costly failure.

Place yourself in the role of recipient. When you receive a mailing shot, why and when do you read it – and buy?

As with all letter-writing, the look of the envelope must be correct for the purpose. You must consider the colour, the quality and the style of address.

If you are writing to a company, then whom should you be trying to reach? Is it the managing director, the company secretary or the buyer – the works or the shop manager – or whom? As with all selling, you must identify your market – and beam in on the individual who has the authority to place the order.

If you can identify the person by name, then do so – but make sure if you can that you get his name absolutely right.

You may be lucky and have your own list of potential buyers. Perhaps you have built it up from previous business. But remember: people change jobs within organisations and move out to other companies. So even your own lists need frequent cleaning.

Next problem: how do you start your letter? It may be 'Dear Mr Brown' – and if you are using a word processor (see Part 6), then the machine can do the work for you. Otherwise, you may address the shot to the managing director and start your letter: 'Dear Sir' – there are regrettably few women MDs, so you need not worry about the 'or Madam' which you may have to use if, for instance, you are addressing the fashion buyer of a department store.

Dear Colleague . . . Dear Customer . . . Dear Delegate . . . take your pick, with care.

Next: what should you put into the letter and what is better in an enclosure? Basically, the letter should be brief and the accompanying literature contain the detail. The letter must draw the customer's eye and instincts to the enclosure, to the detail – and hopefully, to the order form.

The letter itself should be brisk – and, as always, its first sentence is crucial. Get that wrong and you pronounce the final sentence on the letter. You will have killed off the deal with your own words.

Conversely: get that initial impact right and you have caught the interest of your reader and placed the first foot on the stairway to a sale.

As with all other letters, the first sentence should not only trap attention but encapsulate the purpose of the letter. Tell the reader what you are offering . . . why it is unique . . . tease his eye forward.

The text must be crisp and tailored to the market. Words are your shop window and you dress it accordingly. You would scarcely use the same style for the boardroom as you would for housewives.

If you get stuck, you can pay professional copywriters to prepare your letter. But there are few who do the job really well. Even if they are craftsmen with words, they will know neither the product nor the market as you do. At best, you should do the job yourself and save the cost of the experts – at worst, at least prepare drafts; review their rewrites – and always insist upon seeing a letter in its final form and, if printed, also in proof.

Make sure that your reply card or order form is detachable; that any offer you make is easy to accept; that any reply is kept simple; and that the letter is accurate, well presented and professional. The sales letter must refer to the enclosures – and the higher the aim the more dignified and prestigious the stationery and the wording.

Will the letter work? Why not try a test mailing and find out.

Which lists best suit your purpose? Probably, those which you have yourself built up – old and satisfied customers and friends are the best. Otherwise, try local sources – telephone directory; classified sections; trade directories, town guides; lists which Chambers of Commerce may provide, free or at a fee.

On a national scale, telephone and trade directories; *Kelly's Directory; The Postcode Address File; The Buyer's National Guide;* the *Dunn and Bradstreet Register* are all useful.

The *Kompass Directory* lists mainly CBI members; *The Times Top 1,000* provides details of leading business enterprises – and the *Guide to Key British Enterprises* selects some 10,000 of the same. *The British Middle Market Directory* provides some 13,000 names.

If you are aiming at a specialist market, you will find that most have at least one specialist directory. And professional, learned and other bodies, institutes and societies produce their own registers.

Other markets require other methods – like spotting from the electoral register young people who will be 18 that year – or engagements and marriages from the columns of the local paper.

You may also buy or rent a list from direct mail houses or other specialised organisations. Others will sell you their lists at a fee – or even may allow you to exchange, setting off the loan of your list against their own. At the end of this chapter, we list some of the organisations which can provide you with the help you may need; from whom you may buy directories or lists; or from whom you can at least obtain guidance or quotes.

Remember: direct-mail selling is a highly skilled and competitive affair. Before you launch your own, work out the costing. How much will you have to spend and what return will make the outlay worthwhile? What are the current postal rates and how are they likely to change and what are the maximum sizes and weights of mailing shots?

Again: would it be worth your while arranging for sampling, testing or market research to be carried out for you before you make your investment? Letter-writing on a major scale involves massive potential expense and risk.

The same rules that apply to direct mail in the UK apply also and with even more force to overseas direct mail. The costs are higher.

At home or abroad, then, direct-mail selling is a professionalised art. If you are an amateur, take heed – and advice – before you plunge any part of your fortune into this useful, growing but potentially perilous area of the letter-writer's art.

Useful publications

Sell's Directory of Products and Services (£24)
Sell's Publications Ltd,
Sell's House, 39 East Street, Epsom, Surrey KT17 1BQ
(Tel: Epsom 26376)

Kelly's Manufacturers' and Merchants' Directory (£45)
Kelly's Directories,
Windsor Court, East Grinstead House, East Grinstead,
West Sussex, RH1 1XD
(Tel: East Grinstead 26972)

The Dun & Bradstreet Register
Dun & Bradstreet Ltd,
6-8 Bonhill Street, London EC2
(Tel: 01-628 3691)

The Times Top 1000 (£15)
Times Newspapers Ltd,
16 Golden Square, London W1R 5BN
(Tel: 01-434 3767)

Guide to Key British Industries (1983 edition £130)
Dun & Bradstreet Ltd,
27 Paul Street, London EC2A 4JU

Kompass Register of British Industry and Commerce (£70)
Kompass Publishers Ltd,
Windsor Court, East Grinstead House, East Grinstead,
West Sussex RH1 1XD
(Tel: East Grinstead 26972)

Skinners British Textile Register (£15)
Kompass Publishers Ltd,
Windsor Court, East Grinstead House, East Grinstead,
West Sussex RH1 1XD
(Tel: East Grinstead 26972)

Ryland's Coal, Iron, Steel, Tinplate, Metal, Engineering, Foundry and Allied Trades Directory (£31)
Industrial Newspapers,
Queensway House, 2 Queensway, Redhill, Surrey RH1 1QS
(Tel: Redhill 68611)

List of Commercial Directories (£29 plus VAT)
List of Surveys Ltd,
Bridge House, Station Approach, Great Missenden,
Bucks HP16 9A7
(Tel: Great Missenden 064271)

The Standard Industrial Classification
Her Majesty's Stationery Office (HMSO),
Atlantic House, Holborn Viaduct, London EC1P 1BN
(Tel: 01-583 9876)

The Direct Mail Databook
Gower Publishing Co. Ltd,
Gower House, Croft Road, Aldershot, Hants GU11 3HR
(Tel: Aldershot 331551)

The Postcode Address File
Postal Marketing Department (PMk 2.3)
Postal Headquarters, 22-25 Finsbury Square, London EC2A 1PH
(Tel: 01-432 1620)
(Or contact the Postal Sales Representative at your local head PO)

Useful addresses

The Direct Mail Sales Bureau,
12-13 Henrietta Street, London WC2E 8JJ
(Tel: 01-836 0164)

The British List Brokers Association,
King House, 11 Westbourne Grove, London W2 4UR
(Tel: 01-221 1500)

The Association of British Directory Publishers,
Windsor Court, East Grinstead House, East Grinstead,
West Sussex, RH19 1XB

The Direct Mail Producers Association,
34 Grand Avenue, London N10 3BP
(Tel: 01-883 7229)

International Lists of Companies Ranked by Size

The Fortune World Business Directory (£3.00). This lists the largest 500 industrial companies outside the USA plus 50 of the world's largest banks ranked in order of turnover in dollars.

The Double 500 (£4.00). Published in two parts in May and June each year showing the first 500 and the second 500 of the USA's largest companies.

Both the above are available from: Fortune Magazine, Time-Life Building, New Bond Street, London W1Y OAA. (Tel: 01-499 4080).

The Times 1000 (£16.25 including postage and packing). Includes a list of 500 leading European companies. Available from: Times Newspapers Ltd, 16 Golden Square, London W1R 5BN. (Tel: 01-434 3767).

International directories

Kompass, a comprehensive directory of industry, trade and services elaborately cross-referenced. Company information includes capital, number employed, names of one or more directors, list of activities.
Directories exist for Australia, Belgium, Denmark, Germany, Austria, Finland, France, Holland, Hong Kong, Indonesia, Italy, Japan, Morocco, Norway, Singapore, Spain, Sweden, Switzerland, Taiwan, Thailand.
Available from: Kompass Publishers Ltd, Windsor Court, East Grinstead House, East Grinstead, West Sussex RH1 1XD.

Dun & Bradstreet European Market Guide contains details of line of business and credit appraisal of 300,000 concerns in 19 European countries. Published in three volumes. Also available: *Latin American Guide, South African Market Guide.*
Available from: Dun & Bradstreet Ltd, 27 Paul Street, London EC2A 4JU.

Other useful addresses:

The European Direct Marketing Association (EDMA),
The Secretary, HR Waldmeier, Fuchsenbergstrasse 15,
CH-8645 JONA, SG, Switzerland.

Direct Mail Marketing Association Inc.,
6 East 43rd Street, New York, NY 10017, USA.

51

Secretaries, Dictating Machines –
and Other Aids

When the typewriter and shorthand came in, the art of calligraphy
went out. As an executive's responsibilities increased, so his available
time decreased and the mechanical labour of actually committing his
words to paper was passed to others – secretaries and shorthand
typists.

Then along came the dictating machine, with the audio typist
taking over a major part of the work of the secretary. Result? The
shortage of secretaries increased. So in this paradoxical world, let us
now consider how to make the best use of aids to letter-writing –
human and mechanical alike and alongside.

The art of using a good secretary or even copy or audio typist
depends, of course, upon finding one in the first place. The usual
methods (through agencies and advertising) are well known. An
increasingly modern variation – recommended and used by me – is
the employment of married ladies in their own homes. In many cases
they are self-employed (with all the tax and other benefits brought by
that happy situation). The ladies work in their own time, in between
doing their household and maternal chores. They charge piece rates
or by the hour (rates varying – as usual – according to the nature of
the work, the skill of the worker and the area).

Home secretaries can transcribe from tapes, carry out instructions
upon them (or given by telephone or personally) – in their own homes
and in their own way. By removing the element of control over the

manner in which the work is actually done, the ladies may properly be called self-employed. But if, in doubt check with your accountant.

The result? With the right secretary, excellent and well produced letters – at reasonable rates. If times are slack for you, you pay less. Conversely, the ladies know that when they have to apply themselves to their machines or telephones with more than usual vigour, the pay will be higher. Result? With luck, satisfaction all round.

But of course, the secretary who does not work physically with you can hardly sit at the side of your desk, pencil poised. Metaphorically, you will not be dictating to her. Literally, dictation is impossible. Therefore the dictating machine comes into its own.

To the lyrical pen of this author, the joys of the dictating machine cannot be over-emphasised. First, you can choose your own working time. Bring your machine home nightly (or keep one in your study) and your wife can hardly complain. Do the same to your secretary and even (or, in a sense, especially) if she is willing, you may run into matrimonial storms.

Again, if you choose your machines carefully, you can find many on the market which use the same sized tapes or cassettes or reels on large, immobile, easily operated office units, and small pocket-sized appendages.

Naturally, you need spares. Strangely, the same industrialists and executives, who make certain that spare parts are available for their works machinery are often incredibly mean when it comes to their office equipment. Most dictating machinery nowadays is well engineered and generally reliable. But machines are only man-made and from time to time they collapse. To operate a successful dictating machine system, you must have 'swops' to hand. And, of course, you need to find yourself swift and reliable service engineers.

When choosing the brand of machines for your purpose, versatility (as we have seen) should be a prime attribute. Are there various machines, using interchangeable tapes and the like, available to suit all your needs? Next, is there adequate servicing of that particular brand in your area? Finally, does the make you have in mind use tapes which are suitable for your requirements?

Shop around very carefully before you plump for any particular make. Once you have chosen, the odds are that you are landed with it, probably for ever. Nothing is more aggravating than to have different machines in the same office or group of offices. Secretaries or copy typists fall ill? Then tapes may have to be sent to others for transcription. Machines break down? Then you will want only one set of spares. You will not employ one dictaphone typist for your work alone? Then clearly the machine she uses for transcription must be the same one as is used by everyone else in the office.

So once you start with one machine, probably you will have to follow on. The disadvantages are obvious. But there are advantages, too. You can obtain trial runs . . . test out various types and brands, before you make your decision . . . and when you come to hammer out a deal with the supplier, you will obviously do much better if you are buying in bulk with prospects of a permanent tie, than you would if you were purchasing singly. Major discounts are seldom for the minor customer.

The average office will, of course, have to use both dictating machine and secretary, machine typist, copy typist and shorthand typist. In any event, no typist will mean either very few letters or letters most laboriously written. So, once again, your typewriters must be carefully chosen. But here there is no reason why you should not use many makes and varieties. Large machines and small . . . mobile and portable, immobile and massive . . . each will have its part to play in the transcribing of your correspondence. Are electric machines worthwhile? What about word processors? (See Part 6.) If you can afford the initial outlay and your typists are (or can be) trained to use sophisticated machines, then their added speed and ease of typing make them a good buy – particularly as the end-product generally looks so much more handsome and distinguished. But if you are short of funds – or the secretaries and typists are not equipped to handle them – then there are many, very excellent makes of 'steam machine', at a vast range of prices. Usually, but not always, you get what you pay for, and you pay more for the better machines. Shop around for the best, for your purposes.

What equipment to choose? All depends upon your needs, your pocket and your preference. Recommendation is important. Experience should be a good guide. And for the latest in ideas, the various office equipment journals (sent in most cases at no cost to the recipients) are well worth careful perusal.

So much for the basic equipment of the letter-writer. Now for some hints on its use.

52

Your Friend, the Dictating Machine

There is only one way to make a dictating machine your ally and that is to use it. At first, talking into a microphone and having to flick a switch in order to obtain a replay seems strange, after the ease with which Miss Jones has redone the last paragraph or read back your latest words of wisdom. But encouraged by the knowledge that while you dictate, Miss Jones is busily at work, transcribing that which you did half an hour ago – so that you are getting the productive effort of two people for the price of two – keep trying and you will find the effort progressively less of a trial to you. Just as the happily married man wonders how he ever managed as a bachelor, so the addict of the dictating machine wonders that he ever coped without one.

It is essential, of course, to have the right equipment, in decent working order and (as we saw in the last chapter) adequately supplied with spares.

Whatever machine you use, you will soon acquire your own technique. To write a letter by machine involves practice, above all else. You will gradually find that your ideas fall into proper shape as you go along – in the same way as if you were dictating to a typist.

If the letter is involved and complicated, you should certainly jot down notes (see Chapter 48). If you are blessed with shorthand you may want to rough out the letter fairly fully and then dictate it. At best, the use of a precedent book should, in many cases, enable your dictation to be smooth and unworried. But at worst, remember that it is far better to dictate a draft; to hack it about after typing; and then to redictate – than to use longhand in the first place. Apart from the reduced physical effort involved, the result is generally more satisfactory – and almost invariably less time-consuming. And what has the executive (or, for that matter, the secretary) to offer, other than the product of his time?

Techniques of dictation vary greatly. Some (like me) dictate even the punctuation. Others leave it to the transcribers' skill or imagination. Some dictate slowly, others with great speed. Some are blessed with transcribers who can type consistently from tape, and swiftly. Other typists are slower. But all sophisticated transcribing machines incorporate a flip-back switch, enabling the secretary to rehear sections that she has missed.

The greatest difficulties in transcription generally arise with portable, battery operated machines, when the batteries have become run down. The tape moves progressively slower, as the juice runs out. But playback is at normal speed. Result? 'Pinky and Perky' . . . the executive's voice reduced to unrecognisable squeaks, which may be highly humerous and apposite for a cartoon soundtrack, but which drive an audio typist to distraction. So do try to keep your batteries recharged and well charged.

Naturally, you should speak clearly, and give your instructions with precision. But the nature of the instructions and their extent will depend upon the skill and experience of the lady who will listen to your words. For instance, you should be able to say simply: 'Please see the precedent at page . . . of the Letter-writing Book and adapt it to be sent to Messrs Smith & Co. . . . The amount involved is £300. . . . Omit paragraph four . . . sign off with a paragraph inviting him to lunch . . . and send my greetings to his wife . . .' Or: 'Please use precedent No. 85 in the Letters Book – but you sign it on my behalf. . .'

Again, in some cases you will have to spell out the individual words. 'I spell: Rumpleforth . . . R–U–M (as in mother) –P (as in Peter) – L–E–F–O–R–T–H.' In the course of time, you and the transcriber will come to a tacit (or explicit) understanding.

To be sure that you have clearly expressed your meaning, it is often useful to say: 'I repeat . . .' and then to spell the same, all over again. But if you do not include the words 'I repeat', you cannot blame the girl if she types the same words twice.

Remember that the best typists are very often those who are able to let words flow into one ear and out on paper, with the minimum of conscious thought. There is an old saying that a man may allow the words to go in one ear and out the other – with a woman, they go in one ear and out the mouth. With a good secretary, this joke is highly defamatory. She will be, of course, the soul of discretion, and words will go in her ear and out on paper so if you wish them to blossom with perfection, you must plant them with firmness and accuracy.

One of the greatest risks in using a tape is that, unlike a secretary's notebook, it is so easily rubbed out. There are few experiences more aggravating than to have to redo correspondence because you have forgotten to remove the tape from the machine and have rewound and then redictated. Conversely, for one secretary to transpose from a reel and for the reel then to get into the hands of another typist and to be retyped is time wastage at its worst. At least no girl is likely to type from the shorthand of another. The odds are that she cannot read it.

As for the tape that goes astray and never gets typed at all, that leaves the entire office frantically playing back every reel or cassette they can lay their hands on, in a (probably vain) attempt to trace the missing piece.

So if you operate dictating machines, you must find some system to indicate when a tape has been used and, preferably, how much of it – and when it has been typed. My suggestion? Immediately you intend to dictate no more on to a particular reel, mark it, preferably with pencil or felt-tipped pen. Indicate with your marking the proportion of the reel that has been used (a third, a half, full, or as the case may be) or the number on the indicator. Then, and only then, rewind and remove the tape from the machine. Or put it into its box, with a slip indicating the contents.

You may want to date the tape; to use stickers for marking; or to indicate the letters or other items on the particular tape. What matters is that the tape should be clearly and firmly marked. By all means put it in its box and mark the outside of that – but what matters is that the tape itself should carry the appropriate mark.

Then, after the tape is typed (but not before) the marking should be erased. Remove the tape from the machine; return it to its box or shelf or drawer – and you will know that no marking means no typing to be done, whilst conversely any mark left on means that the reel has not been dealt with. Either way, endless trouble and aggravation is avoided.

Finally, microphone technique. This varies. Some hold the 'mike' close to their lips, others far away. Some clutch it and talk to it as a friend, others leave it lying upon the table. You use your machine and you develop your technique. Once acquired, it will never be forgotten. And the pencil-toting secretary will be a comparative stranger to you. Still, there will be times when you need her. So now let us deal with them.

53

Making the Best of Your Secretary and Shorthand Typist

'She was a good secretary, as secretaries go – and as secretaries go, she's gone!' A common lament – but one which can be avoided, if you bear in mind a few, basic rules – for her comfort, as well as your own.

First, the days when you could dictate to your staff, metaphorically as well as literally, are gone. Dictation should be confined to machine or notebook. Otherwise commands should (unless the girl happens to be a masochist) be phrased with some subtlety. No one would suggest that the executive should woo his secretary, like his wife. But dictation in the office should be performed with sophistication or at least with humanity. However much the divorce laws may be liberalised, the marital union remains a good deal more permanent than the length of the stay of the average secretary, with her executive boss.

In any event, the best place to start using your secretary sensibly and well is in her contract of service – details in Chapter 63. Establish a sensible, fair basis and you need not worry too much about having her 'poached', by competitors in your field or any other. But remember that unless she is induced to break her contract of service with you (by giving insufficient notice), you have no remedy against the man who steals your girl. It is up to you to provide terms and conditions which will induce her to stay on.

Once she has safely arrived on your premises, you may find that she has difficulty in taking your dictation – either by pencil or machine. This does not necessarily signify that she is an ignoramus, an illiterate or a nitwit. While dictating, everyone has a different style. The simple, unconscious tricks which worked so well with the last young lady require explanation to the next. And when it comes to adapting precedents (your own or other people's) to suit your convenience, style and tastes, then while no one can guarantee that your patience will be rewarded, it is an absolute certainty that impatience is likely to cost you a new (and potentially able) employee, even before her time with you has really begun. Bearing in mind the high fees which you will probably have had to pay to your secretarial agency and/or the cost of advertising, the rewards of patience are worth waiting for.

As to dictating-machine techniques, these are covered in the preceding chapter. But what of the man who still wishes to dictate his correspondence to the shorthand typist? What advice have we for him?

Most obviously, the better the girl at her work, the less advice you will need . . . the quicker she can take down . . . the more surely she can read back . . . the easier she can adapt to your whims and ways. But bright or dull, tall or small, sullen or smiling, you must not only make sure that she is well supplied with well sharpened pencils and notebooks to her needs and taste, but that she learns your routine, your style and your methods, as swiftly as possible, according to her capacity. In other words, train her – and cherish her. And make sure that she reads this book, from cover to cover.

WORD PROCESSING

Word Processing and Modern Technology

by David Roth

Do I need a word processor?

It has become almost impossible to pick up a newspaper or trade magazine without being bombarded by numerous companies informing you that the letter-writing in your business would work far more efficiently with the installation of a word processor. Do not get carried away with the wonders of modern technology without sparing many thoughts as to whether a word processor in your business will live up to the advertiser's dream.

Whether a word processor is right for your organisation depends entirely on the type of work that forms the majority of your typing load. A word processor with its numerous features will barely speed up the day-to-day ordinary correspondence – though it may make corrections easier, which can in any event be done relatively easily with a self-correcting electronic typewriter.

On the whole, the most effective use of a word-processing system is for repetitive work, where sections of the text are used in several different documents. These can be installed in the memory and subsequently slotted into the appropriate sections of a particular document, which avoids the constant retyping of practically identical or identical copy. The word processor also has the added bonus of allowing the printing of many perfect copies with minor changes, e.g. a different address, name, final sentence, etc., in a fraction of the time it would take using a normal typewriter.

By far the most common uses for a word processor are standard letters; reports; legal documents; records; proposals; manuals; and mailing lists.

Standard letters

Standard letters are used for all sorts of occasions from reminder letters on overdue accounts to personalised mailing shots or for advertising or marketing. The standard part of the text of the letter is printed out and the system automatically merges the names and addresses, which are stored in the machine, and inserts these at the appropriate points in the text.

Reports and legal documents

If you produce long reports which then go through a number of draft stages, a word processor will save you and your secretary much proof-reading and retyping time. The first draft is typed into the word processor, a copy printed out and a record of the report stored in the computer's memory. The author then corrects, edits and adds to the draft in his usual way. He then returns it to his secretary who recalls the draft back onto the computer screen and keys in the corrections as required. The printer then prints out either another draft (some systems print a symbol in the margin or mark the text in some way, indicating the alterations, to speed up the final checking), or a final report with a change in the typestyle, spacing and layout, if required. This has advantages both to the typist and to the author, the main ones being:

1   Only the corrections need to be typed in again – the remaining text is untouched and so does not have to be retyped and therefore rechecked.
2   The author can make changes which previously would have caused a retype, and still get his work returned quickly. For example, he can insert new sections or paragraphs or delete unwanted ones or refine existing text. The typist spends much of her time typing new words into the machine rather than retyping old ones. The author can obtain a high-quality result remarkably quickly.

Updating

Word processors will benefit any company which has text needing frequent updating e.g. salesmen's manuals and price lists, brochures, or mailing lists. Only the changes will need to be retyped.

When is a word processor not a word processor?

If you are not already confused by the time you have made a few preliminary enquiries, you will certainly end up thoroughly perplexed by the many different word-processing facilities and machines available. So to help you, here is a brief introduction to what a word processor is and the different forms it takes.

Whatever word processor you are considering, it will include the basic components which make up every unit: a keyboard similar to a normal typing keyboard for inputting information; a printer for printing out the final result; an internal memory, for storing text, on some form of magnetic storage, either tapes or disks; and a working memory. Nowadays, all models have visual display units (VDUs) somewhat like a normal TV screen, which vary in size, displaying from one line of text to a whole page. This enables text to be seen as it is being typed in, or as called up from the magnetic memory to be corrected and edited before the final printing takes place. The computer world has yet to standardise its terminology for the various types of word processors, but in general there are four:

The 'standard' word processor

This is a totally self-contained system with only one keyboard to input text. It is sometimes known as a 'dedicated' word processor, as it is generally impossible to change its function (see Figure 1).*

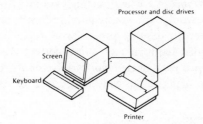

Figure 1 *Stand-alone dedicated word processor*

'Shared logic' system

This has several keyboards which are connected to a computer containing all the memory and logic. The printers can also be shared. Terminals in this type of system are completely unintelligent, which means that if the central computer unit fails to work, for

*Figures 1–4 are taken, with kind permission, from H. Harris and E. Chauhan, *So You Want to Buy a Word Processor?*, Business Books, 1982.

whatever reason, the operating stations attached to it are consequently made inactive (see Figure 2).

Distributed logic systems

These have a central storage unit with shared printers. They have the advantage of having intelligent terminals, each with at least a working memory of its own and sometimes limited external storage so that work can continue for some time if the central processing unit fails to function (see Figure 3).

Word processing on computers

There has been a vast increase in the number of word-processing packages available for micro- and minicomputers. This could well be a solution if you do not have enough suitable work to justify a word processor full time, as you would be able to combine other facilities with it, such as your accounts, invoicing or stock control.

Storage

How much a word processor can store and the extent of its facilities are of great importance. Very few machines are easy to expand if you underestimate the storage size you require. In some cases it may well mean you have to buy another processor or replace 'software' to fulfil your expanded requirements – so a correct choice from the outset can save you a great deal of money and embarrassment. Word processor storage facilities basically fall into three categories (see Figure 4):

1   The $5\frac{1}{4}$-inch mini floppy disk;
2   The 8-inch standard disk;
3   The (Winchester) hard disk;

and as if this is not enough, a new size is now coming onto the market.

In principle, the larger the disk the greater the capacity for storage. A single-density mini floppy disk stores about 30–35 pages of A4 text; a double-density mini floppy disk about 63–67 A4 pages; a single-density 8-inch disk about 100 A4 pages; a double-density 8-inch disk – double that, whilst a hard disk stores about 3,500 A4 pages.

The hard disk, as well as having a higher storage capacity, is about ten times as fast as any of the other systems in accessing information

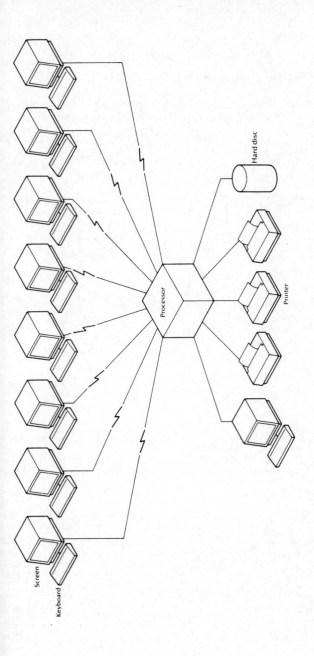

Figure 2 *Shared logic system*

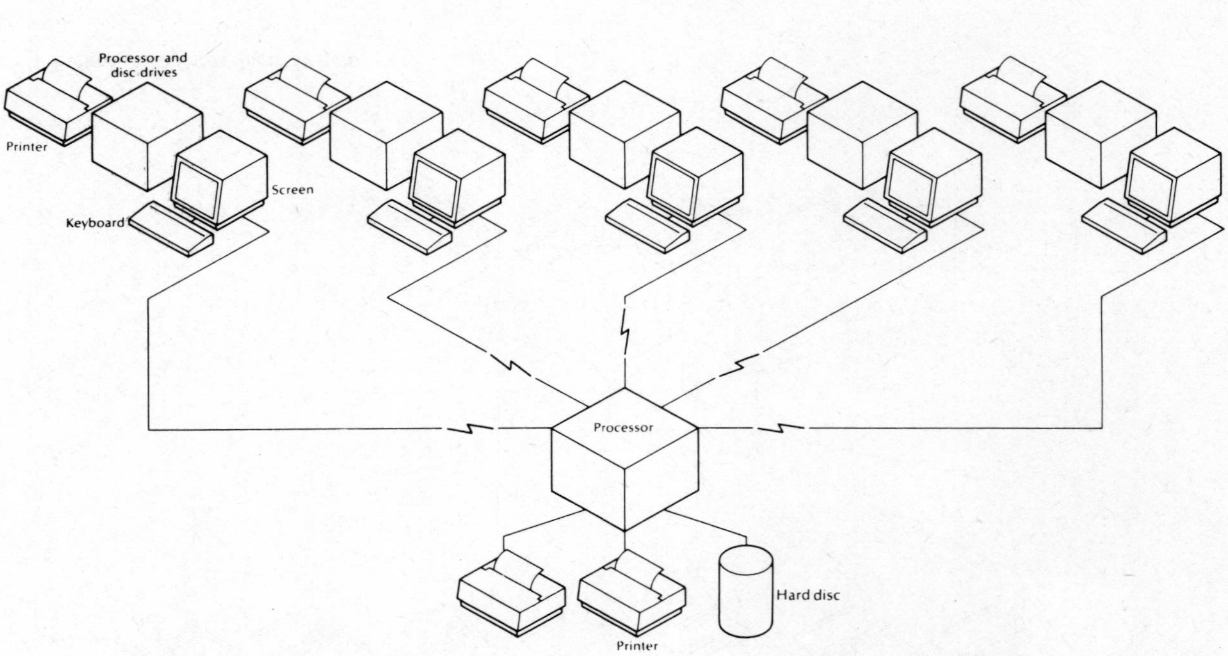

Figure 3 *Distributed logic system*

Printer

Procesor and disc drives

Screen

Keyboard

Processor

Hard disc

Printer

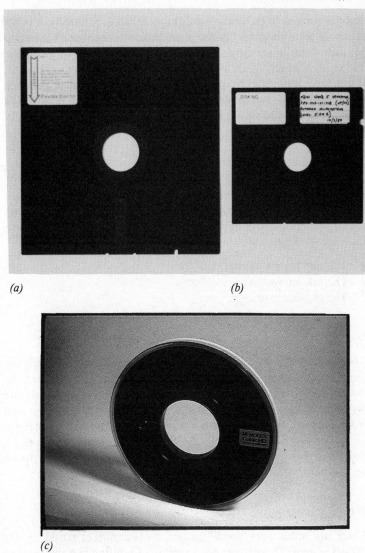

(a) *(b)*

(c)

Figure 4 *Floppy disks:* (a) *8-inch;* (b) *5½-inch;* (c) *hard (Winchester)*

and has proved to be on the whole more reliable. Naturally, it is not cheap. If your budget is limited, your choice lies between 8-inch and 5¼-inch disks. Some elementary calculations on your own workload will show whether 5¼-inch disks are too small for your requirements. If you have reports to be typed which are longer than 60 pages, then the 5¼-inch disk will have its disadvantages. This is a question of economics, but you would be well advised to take a long-term view of your typing requirements.

The printer

There is no point in saving text and editing it only to be able to view it on your screen. So a printing device is essential. The type of printer which you choose will again depend largely on the application you have for it. There are three types of printer available:

1 The dot matrix printer.
2 The ink-jet system.
3 The character printer.

Dot matrix printers

The dot matrix printer works by a series of small needles hitting the paper to form characters. They are reasonably fast and can be cheap but do give a rather 'dotty' appearance. Whilst this is very adequate for internal use, it is less sharp and clear than a type now expected from a normal typewriter with a carbon ribbon, though some high-quality ones are now available. So where a letter needs to look as if it has been personally typed, a dot matrix printer is unlikely to be acceptable.

Ink-jet systems

There are some very good printers on the market based on the ink-jet system. These have the capability of printing in different type faces, as well as complicated graphics. However, as you would expect, they are significantly more expensive than matrix and character printers.

Character printers

The 'character printer' is the printer needed for high-quality type, but it has two drawbacks. It is much slower than the matrix printer; and it is more expensive – costing from around £1,000 upwards.

Whichever printer you decide on, its most important other characteristic is its speed. In computer terminology this is measured in the characters per second (cps) the printer is able to print. The most common character printer speeds are between 45 and 55 cps. Some cheaper printers only print at 40 cps down to 15 cps. Such a slow speed is likely to cause an unacceptable bottleneck and can easily cut the productivity of your word processor by well over 50 per cent.

Some advertising literature quotes character speeds in words per minute. This is generally done to cover up the slow speed at which the printer works. It is totally meaningless, unless you know how long the particular words they are printing are. So go and watch the printer in which you are interested, in full operation.

If you intend to print a lot of standard letters or long reports, you will probably need an *automatic single-sheet feeder* on your printer. This is a device which clips onto your printer to enable it to take about 200 sheets of paper and feed them into the printing carriage one at a time without any manual assistance. If you do need this facility, be sure that the printer in which you are interested is able to take one as not every printer can. Currently, these are unrealistically expensive and add between £500 and £800 to the printer price.

When purchasing a printer, you must remember that it is the speed at which it prints a page that has the greatest effect on the amount of work that it can handle in a day. For example, a 55 cps printer will take 2 hours less on a day's work than one running at 35 cps. A speed of less than 45 cps should only be considered if workload for the word processor will never exceed half a working day.

So choose your printer with the utmost care and attention. A wrong choice could lead to a frustratingly slow volume of work output and cause you and your organisation tremendous difficulties.

Maintenance and after sales

Once you have purchased your computer, you should receive the same attention from the seller's representatives as you did prior to the contracts being signed. The supplier should provide a degree of free training to you as the user, though this varies considerably from supplier to supplier. Ideally, provision should be made so that training will continue for some time after installation on, say, a one-day-a-month basis – though operators' needs do vary. Your word processor should also include a well documented manual explaining the entire system and all its commands, together with examples.

When your word processor is installed and in full operation, a breakdown is likely to cause severe disruption to your workflow. If the machine is new, you may have two remedies:

1   The agreement with the seller may give you express rights – either against the seller or under a 'guarantee' or 'warranty' against the manufacturer.

2   In the event, the Sale of Goods Act gives you in general a right to a word processor which is 'of merchantable quality' – that is, not defective – and 'reasonably suitable for the purpose supplied'. It is most unlikely that any clause excluding those rights would be upheld. If you are a private buyer, then any such clause would be void; and even in a business contract, a court may hold such a clause to be 'unfair' or 'unreasonable' and hence unenforceable.

So if your machine breaks down you should be entitled to require the seller to put it right. In theory, you should not need, at least initially, a maintenance contract at an additional charge. You may well be asked to pay between 10 and 15 per cent of the purchase price for a year's maintenance. But why should you pay this in order to get defects remedied which should not have been there in the first place?

However, some people do take out a contract to avoid potential legal hasle. If you do want a service agreement, either from the beginning or when the machine needs maintaining or repairing as a result of 'fair wear and tear', see where you can get the best deal.

Some suppliers offer a replacement machine; others do not. You should expect a normal response time to breakdowns to be within 24 hours.

Be careful that the maintenance contract does not commit you to obtaining consumer durables such as ribbons, disks and replacement print heads. There are now many alternative sources of supplies and you do not want to be tied down to any one supplier or to his prices. Specialist consumables suppliers may charge as little as half as much as equipment suppliers.

Like any good insurance policy, your annual maintenance contract charge may be high but the risks involved in not having one are usually greater. Many engineering companies will charge a high fee to service a machine not covered by a maintenance contract.

Remember: if the machine which you rely upon breaks down, especially in a busy period, the result could be disastrous, so you will not only need facilities for prompt maintenance, but possibly a back-up machine available during the repair period.

Do your word processors need a special environment?

Gone are the days when computers required a room to themselves, special lighting, highly sophisticated air conditioning, and the like. Technology does not require such elaborate settings. Still, some environmental aids will help in the smooth running and implementation of your word processor.

Lighting

To get the best definition from the screen, lighting should be less bright than normal and should not shine directly onto the screen. Place the work station so as to avoid any reflections from nearby windows or from direct overhead lighting. Each desk should have its own lighting which can be adjusted by the operator to best advantage. Should glare be unavoidable, you can buy a variety of anti-glare filters and screens.

Desks

The desks used for the VDUs should ideally be of a matt finish and should be adjustable by the operator.

Static electricity

Static electricity is a major problem with electrical equipment. So a carpet with built-in anti-static treatment should be used, or existing carpets should be treated with anti-static spray.

Build-ups of static electricity have been blamed for system black-outs and the loss of information stored in disks, so elimination of static electricity is vital.

Power supply

The power supply connected to the word processor should be direct, i.e. a *direct* contact to the main electricity supply. Other office machinery on the same supply could upset the stability of power to the word processor and cause untoward damage.

Noise

Printers are noisy even if fitted with an acoustic soundproof hood (which is strongly recommended). So noise should be minimised by careful positioning of the printers, and perhaps used with screens or soundproof partitioning.

Some word processors have silent keyboards. These are not advised as it has been proved that operator mistakes increase when keyboards make no sound at all. Some keyboards have adjustable noise levels where the operator can choose whichever noise level is preferred.

To buy, lease or rent?

Whether you should buy your own word processor or enter into a leasing agreement with one of the finance houses depends on your business and your ready cash.

When a leasing or rental arrangement is entered into, the computer is or becomes the property of the leasing company. Depending on the contract, you may have an option to buy the machine at a pre-agreed price when the lease expires. This has the advantage that you do not have to lay out so much capital and with renting the agent is responsible for maintenance. At the end of the leasing period you have an option either to buy your existing machine or to carry on another agreement for a more up-dated and sophisticated version. Many bureaux now offer word-processing facilities though these would probably not be cost-effective if you are only going to use their services for word processing.

Whichever system of payment you enter into, either buying outright or leasing, you should discuss it with your accountants. They may have other suggestions as to the most beneficial and cost-effective way of acquiring capital equipment for your business.

How to assess your word-processing requirements

Word-processing salesmen, like all others, are not renowned for giving unbiased advice. Especially in the crazy world of microelectronics, it is all too easy to become bemused and confused with the technical marvels of numerous facilities that salesmen will insist your company cannot do without. Avoid this confusion and avoid acquiring a machine with a host of technical features that will be of no benefit to you. Here is how.

Discuss the needs of your organisation with your colleagues. You *must* define exactly what it is you want your word processor to do and prepare a detailed specification. This should include all the specific needs of all your various departments as well as the normal general requirements.

Here is an outline of the various questions you should be asking to prepare your specification:

1 What are the sizes of your longest documents, the frequency at which they occur, and the quantity of standard or semi-standard letters you wish to produce and the number of typewriters you wish to replace?

2 Do you want the word processor to produce standard letters, such as mailshots, with circulars to customers, etc.? If so, how many names have you on your mailing list? How much does your list increase each year? How many letters will be produced each week or each month? Will each letter go to everyone on the list, or is the word processor expected to select names by area, type of business, turnover or by any other factor?

3 Do you require the word processor to be used for the production of your reports and manuals? If so, how many pages will the longest documents contain? Is automatic typing of page numbers, page headings and page footings required? Do you need the word processor to generate the contents of pages automatically? How many draft versions do you generally produce of a booklet before the final version is approved and ready to be circulated?

4 What sort of screen display do you need? Do you want a single line, a conventional 24 lines or a full page? Do you prefer brown, green, black or white characters? Do you want the keyboard and screen to be compact and portable so that the typist can use a space at her desk for other purposes when she is not using the word processor? Or do you want the space to be permanently devoted to word-processing activities?

5 What is the total volume of printing, in terms of pages per week,

that you already type? Is this likely to increase in the coming months or years?

6   What sort of paper are you going to print on? Will it be continuous stationery or single sheets? If it is to be single sheets, do you need an automatic single-sheet feeder to the printer?

7   Do you need to have a system that can print one document whilst the operator is typing another document?

8   Is the volume of expected word processing enough to exceed one keyboard operator? If so, will you buy a separate word processor for each typist or do you want a system that has the ability to link several terminals to one word processor? Do you require more than one printer? If so, do you need a word processor which can drive several printers simultaneously?

9   Do you require your new system to do other tasks in addition to plain word processing? For example, some systems are now able to punch telex tapes, communicate with large computers or other word processors, or have facilities for payroll ledgers, stock control, invoicing, etc.

Once you have answered these questions with your colleagues, you will be in a better position to sort out the type of word processor that you require and will be able to have better idea of the price range of your requirements. It is worthwhile even at this stage to take into account the running costs of consumables that you will need for your word processor. If you use a carbon ribbon, a word-processor printer can use up to one ribbon per 45 minutes of printing. If your work amounts to four hours of printing per day, you will use 20 ribbons per week; at a cost of about £4–7 per ribbon (depending upon whether you buy them in bulk) taking the lowest figure, this gives ribbon costs of about £70 per week or £3,500 per year.

How to approach the word-processing dealer

After having identified your needs, you should contact a variety of suppliers of word-processing machines, from the well known multinational to the small word-processing shops which are becoming commonplace in most High Street shopping centres. It costs you only the time to visit them or to ask their representative to come to you, to see what solutions they can offer for your particular word-processing application.

You should have your drawn-up requirement specification accessible and in such a form that you can go down the list with the prospective supplier and tick off the facilities that his machine provides.

After having heard about four or five systems *and seen them demonstrated,* you will soon become confused as to which one does what. Doing it in this way will enable you quickly to see which system offers the best of the facilities that you require. No system is perfect, but some will be far better than others for your application. Despite what the salesmen may tell you it is your application that counts. Even if a particular system has magnificent facilities, they will be useless to you if you do not need them.

To help you prepare this document, here is a checklist. It is inevitably incomplete as it will vary with the nature of your application, but it does contain all the basics which you should look for in your word-processing machine.

Creation of a document

a Automatic tab which will allow left- or right-hand indenting of text.
b The ability to set several different sets of margins within a single document.
c Right-hand margin justification and realignment of text to new left- or right-hand margins.
d Required-join facility so that the processor will not split up text if it comes to the end of a line, e.g. a hyphenated company name or date.
e Facility for producing graphics.
f Facility to line text automatically to decimal points or commas.
g Facility to underline specified sections of the text automatically.
h Facility to centre text between margins automatically.
i Facility to have at least 200 characters' width on a document.
j Facility to title in capital letters and underline them.

Editing

The following facilities:

1 To delete text either by character, word, line, paragraph, or entire page.
2 To insert a small or large amount of text at any point in a document without altering the text preceding or following the insertion.
3 To print the text in two or more columns on one page.
4 To erase, underline, or enhance from text by character, word, line, paragraph, or page.
5 To automatically number and renumber pages of a document.
6 To move text on same page by means of 'walking' up and down the screen.
7 To amend one document to any position in another document on the screen and therefore create a new document.
8 To automatically modify or replace a word or string of text every time it appears in a document.

Printing

The following facilities:

a To print from the screen or from a designated file.
b To print out a document with different line spacing or margins from the original document.
c To choose from 10-, 12-, or 15-pitch, as well as proportional spacing.
d To use both standard paper and continuous stationery paper.
e To attach an automatic sheet feeder.

Solving the problems

Having decided to introduce a word processor to your business, work out well in advance the probable effects that introduction may have. Formulate a policy to decide what is to be done to solve the likely problems. While the problems will differ vastly from business to business, those listed below are the most common ones so easily forgotten, with potentially disastrous results:

1 What will happen to already existing individual secretaries if some of their workload is assigned to the word processor? What are the industrial relations implications?
2 Will the word-processor operators be selected from your existing staff or specially hired for the word processor?

3 Who will train the operators initially and their eventual replacements?

4 As it is difficult to get temporary operators – what will happen and how will you cover when your operator is ill or away on holiday? Will the word-processing unit have to close down?

5 How will the remuneration of your word-processing operator be linked to that of other typists?

6 How will you train the authors of text that goes into the word processor to the capabilities of the machine and how to obtain the best results?

As word processors can achieve far more in a day than many typists with ordinary typewriters, losing one operator for whatever reason may have the same effect as losing several typists with a traditional machine. Trained temporary staff are hard to obtain and with the vast amount of different systems and machines available on the market, the chances of finding one capable of running your system is slim.

Buying a word processor is like getting married – whether it is the right decision or not you are stuck with it for some time to come, so, like marriage, great thought and consideration need to be taken before making the final purchasing decision. A word processor can easily be a lethal weapon in the wrong hands and, if wrongly chosen, can quickly bring the parts of your organisation that it affects to a grinding and resounding halt. Where big amounts are involved, it is advisable to engage the services of a professional, *independent* computer consultant to advise you on the purchase of a system. After all where large sums are involved in percentage terms the amount paid to consultants is very small and could save both you and your company a great deal of embarrassment. As well as being involved in the initial purchase of a machine, your consultant should be retained to take you through the transition period and to ensure that the supplier supplies a machine and system which is fully operational when installed in your premises.

'. . . and a letter to Acme Office Supplies Ltd, cancelling the order for the dictating machine . . . .'

Part 7

THE LAW ON LETTERS

Introduction

The letterwriter cannot avoid contact with the law. Hence the companion volumes to this book. Hence, too, the following chapters, which set out the law that the letterwriter is most likely to meet.

First, there are those laws which apply specifically to letters – the legal results of signing a document; the possible effects of carelessness in what you write; copyright; defamation; and other legal traps.

Next, there are certain branches of the law which the letterwriter most commonly requires. We deal, for instance, with contracts in general and contracts of employment in particular. Finally, suing for the money you are owed; problems in court; and letters in dispute.

For more detailed coverage of the law explained in this book, you may care to refer to one of my more specific books, listed at the front of this one. I am only sorry that I cannot condense the entire legal package into the pages that follow. But if the commercial letterwriter follows the legal rules set out in those pages, he should not go far wrong.

55

Copyright

The ownership of a letter passes from the writer to the recipient. The letter you receive becomes your property. You may file it or tear it up, treasure it or give it away. But you are not entitled to copy it. Copyright remains in the writer. You cannot include it in your memoirs without the writer's permission. A book of precedents, such as the companion volumes to this one, is made to be copied by businessmen, for their everyday correspondence – but not by other authors or lawyers, for their own books. The laws of copyright, then, are vital to the letterwriter. Here they are, as you are most likely to meet them.

Naturally, you will make use of your own knowledge, skill and experience, when writing, drawing, or preparing office precedents.

But otherwise, you may rely upon the brain-children of others. How far can you do so without running into the laws of copyright?

Copy one man's work, goes the old saying, and that's cheating. Copy more than one man's efforts – and that's research! Well, so far as the law is concerned, if you copy something in which copyright subsists, you are liable to be sued for infringement of copyright – and the more people's work you copy, the more potential plaintiffs you are creating. In daily, office practice, however, we all work from precedents . . . either for ourselves or for others, we have to copy. Indeed, with modern, sophisticated machinery and equipment, copying becomes daily an easier task. But it has its perils. So consider for a moment, *The Copyright Act 1956.*

Where copyright subsists in any work, you are in general only entitled to copy that work with the licence of the owner. Invent your own precedents; write your own advertising material; draw your own plans, diagrams or maps; create your own instructions to your staff – and you have the right to prevent them from being copied by others, without your consent. But you are only entitled to reproduce the original brain-children of others, with their consent.

Copyright subsists in 'literary, dramatic, musical . . . and artistic works'. These terms cover just about everything, from railway timetables to drawings, maps, charts, plans – and poetry and literature of the highest order. During the author's lifetime and for fifty years from the end of the calendar year in which the author dies, reproduction is usually only allowed with the author's consent. Nor need the reproduction be exact to amount to a 'copy' – 'a copy' is that which comes so near to the original as to give to every person seeing it the idea created by the original. So not only are exact reproductions covered but so are 'colourable imitations'.

Now, 'copyright' means 'the exclusive right . . . to authorise other persons to do . . . acts in relation to that work . . . ', usually in the United Kingdom or countries with reciprocal rights. But who is 'the owner'?

In general, 'the author of a work is entitled to any copyright subsisting in that work'. But there are exceptions.

'Where a literary, dramatic or artistic work is made by the author in the course of his employment by the proprietor of a newspaper, magazine or similar periodical under a contract of service or apprenticeship, and is so made for the purpose of publication in the newspaper, magazine or similar periodical, the said proprietor shall be entitled to the copyright in the work in so far as the copyright relates to publication of the work in any newspaper, magazine or similar periodical, or to reproduction of the work for the purpose of its being so published; but in all other respects, the author shall be entitled to any copyright subsisting in the work by virtue of this part of the Act.'

There is one other exception in the Act. 'Where a person commissions the taking of a photograph, or the painting or drawing of a portrait, or the making of an engraving, and pays or agrees to pay for it in money or monies' worth, and the work is made in pursuance of that commission, the person who so commissioned the work shall be entitled to any copyright subsisting therein . . . .'

If you decide to have your office rebuilt or redesigned and you commission an architect to draw up the plans, he normally retains the copyright. The fact that you commissioned and pay for the work is irrelevant. You are not entitled to take his designs, reproduce them and sell them – or even to reproduce them and keep them. He has the right to decide who may and who may not copy the work.

But if you commission someone to take a photograph of your office or to make a drawing or engraving of it, the Act says that the copyright belongs to you.

All this is subject to agreement to the contrary. There is nothing to prevent you from employing an architect on the basis that you will acquire the copyright in his drawings; nothing, that is except possibly his reluctance to agree to this. Equally, if you employ some talented person in your office on the basis that he shall have the copyright in any original works he produces in the course of his employment, the Act will not remove his right. Like so many pieces of legislation, it only applies in the absence of some agreement to the contrary.

Section 5 lays down how copyright is infringed. You must not 'without the licence of the owner of the copyright . . . sell, let for hire, or by way of trade offer or expose for sale or hire any article or . . . by way of trade exhibit any article in public . . . if to your knowledge the making of the article constitutes an infringement of that copyright . . .' And you must not distribute any article either for the purpose of trade or 'for other purposes, to such extent as to affect prejudicially the owner of the copyright in question . . . '.

There are exceptions. Libraries are given special privileges. So are those who use extracts from works for the purpose of reviews or criticisms. But in general, the rule is simple – literary, musical, artistic and architectural piracy are not permitted.

If you do infringe someone's copyright, the Act gives him specific remedies. First, he is entitled to the same rights in respect of the copies you have made as if he actually owned them. So you may have to hand them over. Second, he can claim from the court an injunction, restraining you from reproducing his work. By all means use your office machines to reproduce the masterpieces of those who own them. But without the permission of the owner of the copyright, you have no right to copy – and the fact that you acted on the instructions of some client will not protect you.

Next, the copyright owner may claim damages. Damages are normally designed in law to compensate the person who has suffered damage. If, for example, you have been supplied with defective office machinery, the damages which you would recover would be the financial loss you had suffered – that is, the cost of putting the machinery into proper order. But the Copyright Act in certain cases allows the owner to claim 'punitive damages' – damages designed not merely to compensate the sufferer but to punish the wrongdoer.

Nor is that all. Anyone who knowingly infringes copyright is guilty of an offence for which he may be fined and, in certain circumstances, imprisoned. Copyright law is not merely designed to protect copyright owners, but is regarded as a means of protecting the public itself.

So the next time someone comes into your office with a request that you duplicate, photostat or copy material which does not belong to him, spare a thought for the Copyright Act. If in doubt, discuss the matter with your client or customer – maybe he has not considered the law. You should not be party to an infringement of copyright.

A final warning. Authors have their own little tricks to prevent their work from being copied. To be more precise, many authors have developed special ways of recognising their work. The right to prevent copying is essential to those who produce original literary, artistic, dramatic, or musical work. Architects, writers, designers, draughtsmen, surveyors, scientists, businessmen who draw up plans, industrialists who own books of data and research . . . they all need the protection of the Copyright Act. And most of them have little hesitation in invoking its protection, if and when their copyright is infringed. So those whose office work includes the reproduction of works of others should beware.

56

Defamation – the Laws of Libel and Slander

It is defamatory to publish anything about another person which would tend 'to lower him in the eyes of right-thinking people'. You must not bring others into 'hatred, ridicule or contempt'. To defame someone in writing or some other permanent form (including, incidentally, a statement made on radio or television) is a libel. To speak ill of another is slander. The letterwriter must be aware of both.

The fact that a statement is true does not prevent it from being defamatory. But no one is entitled to a good name which he has not earned. So, if sued for a defamatory statement which you can prove to be true, you may plead 'justification'. But the effect of a plea of justification is to repeat again – and even more loudly and publicly – the very same defamatory statement that you made before. Hence if a plea of justification fails, your offence has been severely aggravated. The damages awarded against you will be greatly increased.

A much more helpful defence for most businessmen on many occasions is that of 'qualified privilege'. The law recognises that certain statements must be made, for the public good. People must be entitled to speak their minds. Hence 'privilege'.

No action in defamation will lie in respect of any statement made in a court of law by anyone, whether it be judge, juryman, witness, or counsel. 'Absolute privilege' also attaches to all statements made in Parliament. Legislators must be able to speak without fear of legal reprisal. However malicious, untrue or unjustified a statement made in court or parliament, it can never give rise to a successful defamation action.

Similar privilege attaches to occasions upon which the law recognises that the writer of the statement has a public or private duty to make it and the reader a direct interest in receiving it. For instance, references are business necessities. So the giver of a reference is protected. He is under a moral duty to speak his mind to the inquirer (although, note, he is under no legal duty whatsoever to supply the reference). The recipient of the reference obviously has an interest in knowing its contents. The occasion is 'privileged'.

Or suppose that you have to write to a senior executive concerning the possible sacking of a member of staff. Your letter alleges that he was dishonest . . . slovenly . . . disobedient . . . stupid . . . unfit to be in your company. He is defamed. But clearly, this sort of letter *must* be written. It contains no mere idle gossip. It is essential company business. The occasion is 'privileged'.

But while the privilege of courts and Parliament is 'absolute', that of the businessman writing or speaking to his colleagues or supplying a reference is 'qualified'. The qualification? That if the statement was made out of 'malice', the privilege evaporates. 'Malice' simply means some wrongful motive. If it can be shown that the object of making the statement was to harm the person defamed rather than to assist the board in coming to a sensible conclusion, or the prospective employer to decide whether or not to employ the person, the privilege goes. The law is not designed to shield the spiteful.

Another defence to the writer of evil words? 'Fair comment on a matter of public interest.' In a country where free speech is treasured, people must be allowed to comment on matters of general concern.

Note, first, that what you write must be a statement of *opinion* and not of alleged *fact*. If the words complained of were partly opinion and partly fact, then in so far as they consisted of fact, they must be substantially correct. Comment to your heart's content, but do not mis-state facts.

The comment must be 'fair'. This does not mean that the recipient or reader or the person named must consider it reasonable. In practice, this word provides little restraint on your comment. Provided you are not simply using the occasion to forward a private grudge rather than to comment on a matter of public interest, you have nothing to worry about. But I repeat: the Englishman's right to comment must not be confused with his continued liability in damages if he confuses fact with fiction and, under the guise of comment, propagates false statements about his enemies.

The writer, then, should watch his words, whenever he is writing evil. Remember the three little monkeys? The one with his hands clapped firmly over his mouth is the most intelligent of all. Speak no evil and you need fear no action in slander.

All this also works, as usual with the law, in reverse. If you are at the receiving end of unkind words, apply these principles and you will know whether, in theory at least, you might have a good action in defamation against the speaker. But do not be surprised if you are advised by your lawyer not to sue, even though an action may lie.

Defamation proceedings tend to be perilous in the extreme. Even if you win, you will endure worry, aggravation and probably expense. While orders for costs are customarily made in favour of winners, these rarely cover all the costs incurred. There is usually a balance over which has to be paid by the winning litigant to his own lawyers, in any event. Nor can defamation proceedings ever be brought with the help of Legal Aid.

Then, of course, your action may go wrong. The lesson of Oscar Wilde should be read by all potential plaintiffs in defamation actions.

Then there was the case of the leading plastic surgeon who was defamed in print by an erstwhile colleague. He sued. Juries have almost entirely disappeared from the civil courts, but they still remain in defamation proceedings. In the plastic surgeon's case, the first jury failed to agree. The case had to be retried. The second jury failed to agree. Once again, the worry, nervous strain and expense recommenced. Only on the third round did the plaintiff win. It was a handsome victory but the cost in frayed nerves and sleepless nights was extreme and the financial risk quite staggering.

57

Sedition, Injurious Falsehood and Other Written Traps

There are various other ways in which the law interferes with freedom of speech or writing. They are all comparatively uncommon in practice, but still require a weather eye from the letterwriter. So here is a miscellany of civil and criminal consequences which can arise out of use of the wrong word.

The offence of 'sedition' embraces 'all those practices, whether by word, writing or deed, which fall short of high treason but directly tend or have for their object to excite dissatisfaction or discontent . . . to create public disturbance, or to lead to civil war . . . to bring into hatred or contempt the sovereign or the government, the constitution or the laws of the realm . . . to excite ill-will between different classes of the sovereign's subjects . . . to incite people forcibly to obstruct the execution of the law . . .' and so on, and so on.

In theory, this offence may put a heavy rein on free, political discussion. But in practice, it, too, is almost as dead as the proverbial dodo.

Not so perjury. If any person who is 'lawfully sworn as a witness or as an interpreter in a judicial proceeding wilfully makes a statement material in that proceedings which he knows to be false or does not believe to be true . . .' he is a perjurer and may be imprisoned for up to seven years or fined an unlimited amount – or both. So when appearing before any 'tribunal, court or person having by law power to hear, examine and receive evidence on oath', mind what you say. And remember that written, sworn evidence must be as accurate as you can make it (see Chapter 58 on Affidavits).

Although there are prosecutions for perjury, bearing in mind the number of perjurers, it is obvious that the fear of committing this offence has about as little effect on the dishonest witness as any terror of purgatory, caused by flouting the witnesses' oath.

Now for some civil results of uncivil words.

As we have seen in the last chapter, defamation may lead to trouble. But has it occurred to you that to speak ill of a person's *goods* may be defamatory of his person? Suppose, for instance, that you say: 'Jones is turning out really shoddy stuff these days and selling it at a very high price'. You are hardly heaping compliments on Jones's goods – but you are saying, in effect: 'That man Jones is a rogue – he is selling low-quality goods at a high price'.

Apart from libel and slander, words may themselves give 'a cause of action' if they cause damage to a person 'in the conduct of his affairs' or are calculated to cause him pecuniary loss.

Suppose, first, that any sort of property is up for sale. A man 'without lawful motive' untruly writes that the property is charged, or that there are liabilities upon it, or that the vendor is not in a position to sell. This is 'slander of title'.

Again, if you write of someone that he is selling goods in infringement of copyright or patent, you may be alleging 'slander of title.' But nowadays, there are various statutory remedies available to people accused of this sort of behaviour (as by section 65 of *The Patents Act 1949* – which says that a person who is threatened with proceedings for infringement of the patent may bring an action for a declaration that the threats are unjustifiable, and may also claim an injunction and, if he has suffered any loss, for damages also).

Again, falsely and maliciously to disparage the quality of a man's goods may create a 'cause of action' – if the disparagement prevents their sale. By all means indulge in 'mere trade puffery', but 'knocking' may lead to trouble.

So where a false statement is made maliciously (out of a desire to injure and without lawful authority) and produces as its direct consequence 'damage which is capable of legal estimation', an action may lie for slander of title, slander of goods 'or other malicious falsehood'.

Finally, just a note on 'malice'. 'Maliciously' has been defined as meaning 'without just cause or excuse'. Unlawfully and intentionally to do 'without just excuse or occasion' an action which causes damage may lead to trouble. But it is certainly malicious to act out of some improper or dishonest motive or with the intention of causing injury. Where there is 'a distinct intention to injure the plaintiff apart from honest defence of the defendant's own property', an action may lie, without there being any defamation as such. (For 'malice' as affecting the defence of 'qualified privilege', see last chapter.)

So, if you improperly or dishonestly attack the title or property or products of your competitors, they may have a good claim against you. The law approves of competition but frowns upon the more unpleasant forms of 'knocking' the goods and property of others.

58

Affidavits and Oaths

An affidavit is a statement of fact, sworn by the 'deponent'. If on conscientious grounds the witness declines to take an oath, then he may make the appropriate declaration. What matters is that the court then has a document made by the witness, presumably as a result of careful thought and, if necessary, research. He is undertaking to tell the truth. If he lies, he is a perjurer.

Far too many affidavits are made far too carelessly. Suppose, for instance, that you want 'summary judgement' – you have issued a writ; there is no apparent defence (or 'triable issue') so your solicitors ask the court to give swift, sharp judgement, without the necessity of a trial. An affidavit will have to be filed, verifying the facts in the writ and saying that there is no defence (or no defence to that part of the claim in respect of which summary judgement is sought).

The affidavit may be sworn by the solicitor. It is then for him to make sure that he is satisfied as to the truth of his assertion or as to the 'information and belief' to which he deposes. But he may provide you with the draft document and ask you take it to a Commissioner for Oaths and have it sworn.

Even if the solicitor has had the document handsomely and apparently permanently typed on special 'engrossing' paper, this should not deter you from perusing every word with care. After all, morality apart, the other side may not cave in; the case may reach trial; if it does, the odds are that you will have to give evidence. If you end up in the witness-box, you will be cross-examined on the basis of your sworn affidavit. A mistake can be very expensive indeed. Take care what you say. Mind your words – particularly when they are written and sworn.

58

The Effect of a Signature

A businessman's handshake may no longer be his enforceable bond. But his signature still means a great deal.

If you sign a letter put before you by your secretary or assistant or executive and (because you rely upon his honesty or skill or judgement) you sign without reading it, please do not think that you will afterwards be able to avoid the legal results of your letter, at least in so far as third parties are concerned. You will be bound by it. That is the major effect of the famous decision in the case of *Gallie* v. *Lee*.

Mrs Gallie was a lady in her 80s. She had a trusted nephew named Walter Parkin, who had been kind to her over the years. He was sole beneficiary under her will and a few years ago, she decided to give him her house: 'Everything I possessed belongs to him', she said. He wanted to raise money on the house and she was willing for him to do so, provided that she could stay in it during her lifetime.

Unfortunately, Mr Parkin had a friend called Lee. He needed money to pay off *his* creditors. On the advice of a solicitor's managing clerk (who was thereafter imprisoned), Lee arranged for documents to be drawn up by which Mrs Gallie would sell the house to him for £3,000. This Lee would not pay, but would mortgage the property.

Lee then prevailed upon Mrs Gallie to sign the document. Unfortunately, her glasses were either mislaid or broken and she did not read what she was signing. 'What is it for?', she asked Mr Lee. 'It is a deed of gift for Wally for the house', Lee replied. She signed. Lee paid her nothing. The solicitors got him a £2,000 loan from the Anglia Building Society. Lee raised money on a second mortgage, but defaulted on the instalments. The Building Society sued for possession. Mrs Gallie and her nephew pleaded *non est factum* – that the document was not hers.

Mere mistakes in the contents of a document you sign will never allow you to avoid its effect. If you are aware of its essential nature, then it is yours, even if the contents are not as you think. However, if the document is entirely different in character and nature from that which you believed you were signing, you may be able to establish that it has no effect.

What, then, of Mrs Gallie's gift?

'A man who has failed to read a document and signs it should not be allowed to repudiate it as against an innocent purchaser,' said Lord Denning. 'His remedy is against the person who deceived him.' Even if he could plead fraud or mistake as against the immediate party (that is, the person who induced the signature of the document), he would not be able to avoid it 'when it had come into the hands of one who had in all innocence advanced money on the faith of it being his document, or had otherwise relied on it . . .'

The principle? 'Whenever a man of full age and understanding who can read and write signs a legal document put before him for signature which on its face is intended to have legal consequences, then, if he does not take the trouble to read it but signs it as it is, relying on the word of another as to its character or effect or contents, he cannot be heard to say it is not his document.'

Lord Justice Russell agreed. Mrs Gallie, he said, had intended to sign a document divesting herself of her interest in the house. This she had done. Here was no case of *non est factum*. Lord Justice Salmon agreed. A court, he said, 'thus achieves a result which accords with reason and justice'.

In the course of their decisions, both Lord Justice Russell and Lord

Justice Salmon made it clear that, in their views, the Court of Appeal is bound by precedent. Unlike the House of Lords, which can now depart from its own decisions, the Court of Appeal is in no such happy position.

So mind what you sign won't you? And if anyone tries to say that he did not realise what he was signing, then just refer him or his solicitors to the case of *Gallie* v. *Lee** and that should be the last you hear of that bad argument.

60

Negligence – and Those Who Write Without Due Care

To drive without due care is an offence dealt with by a criminal court. If someone else suffers damage as a result of a careless statement, it may lead to trouble all round. That was one effect of an important decision of the House of Lords.

A well known merchant bank was asked for a reference. The inquirers wished to know whether a certain company was worthy of credit. The bank supplied the information; and when this turned out to be incorrect the inquirers lost their money. They sued the bank, claiming that although they (the inquirers) were not customers and the information was supplied gratuitously, the bank still 'owed them a duty of care ' – that is, was under a duty to them to exercise such care as was reasonable in all the circumstances to ensure that the information given was correct.

'Nonsense', retorted the bank. 'We supplied the service at no charge and you cannot expect us to have the same liability to you as we would have had, if you were a customer or we had charged you. And anyway,' they added, 'there was a disclaimer on the reference saying that it was given "without responsibility" on the part of the bank or its officers.' And they denied negligence.

The trial judge held that they had been negligent but that the effect

---

*The Court of Appeal's decision was affirmed by the House of Lords, where the case was known as *Saunders* v. *Anglia Building Society*.

of the disclaimer was to let them off the hook. They were under a duty of care, even though the service was given gratuitously. This decision was eventually upheld by the House of Lords.

The basic principle was established long ago. We each owe a duty of care to our 'neighbour'. A 'neighbour', in this sense, is any person whom we ought reasonably to anticipate would be likely to be affected by our negligent act. If, then, you are a manufacturer, you have a liability in contract to the people who buy your goods. If the goods are faulty, then you are in breach of contract. If you are negligent and they suffer injury, loss or damage, then you may be held liable.

But your responsibility does not end there. It extends to 'the ultimate consumer'. Suppose that you manufacture drink. It must be obvious to you that the person who is likely to drink it is not the wholesaler or retailer to whom you actually sell the stuff. The man behind the bar may drink some of his brew, but if he drinks it all there will be no profits. The 'ultimate consumer' – the customer of the retailer or caterer – is the man who will be poisoned if the drink is defective. He is the 'neighbour' of the manufacturer.

So there is a liability in the law of negligence not only to those whom you know but even to complete strangers.

'The bank', said the House of Lords, in effect, 'must be taken to have realised that the reference was asked for with a purpose in mind. The intention was that the reference be acted upon. So the bank ought to have realised that if the reference was incorrect, the result might well be that the recipient would suffer damage. So the bank owed a duty of care to that recipient, even though the service was given gratuitously.' The milk of human kindness may prove a very costly commodity.

So negligence had been found against the bank and a duty of care was owed. The damage was also proved. That left the disclaimer. The bank had given the reference upon the explicit and clear understanding that it was not to be held responsible for the accuracy of the document. The recipient could not go behind that disclaimer which was fully effective to protect the bank. As a result, the House of Lords did not have to consider the question of whether the defendants had been guilty of negligence. The bank escaped because of its disclaimer.

Since that decision*, many business people have shivered slightly and taken insurance cover. The giver of every sort of reference must

Hedley Byrne v. *Heller and Partners* (1964).

take care not only to avoid defamation in circumstances in which malice may be imputed to them (see Chapter 56) but must be careful to ensure that, if asked for a reference for one Peter Smith, he does not provide it in respect of another. He owes a 'duty of care' to the recipient.

It is not enough to prove that you were negligent in giving the advice or information concerned. To obtain damages against you, your correspondents would have to prove two other matters: first, that the statement concerned was acted upon; second, that they suffered damage, foreseeably arising from the negligence.

Infallibility being a divine attribute, every businessman makes mistakes. Happily, most of them lead nowhere. Indeed the great advantage of making a mistake is that next time you may recognise it. If others do the recognising, then that is unfortunate. But it is only if they do not realise that you have been in error and actually take action as a result of your mistake that they will have a legal remedy.

Suppose, for instance that you make a misleading statement in a letter. As a result, the recipient consults his board, his solicitor, his accountant, his management consultant and then – bolstered by the expert approval – takes action along the lines you have suggested. The chances are that he could not blame you. There were too many intervening people, facts and ideas.

Alternatively, suppose you make some provocative statement. It may never enter your mind that anyone would be stupid enough to act upon it without further research or inquiry. But maybe you were being obtuse. The question is: Would the 'reasonable man' have expected you to have foreseen that your correspondent would act upon your words? Should you reasonably have prophesied, had you applied your mind to the situation, that your words would give rise to someone else's action? If not, then your mistake will lead nowhere – at least so far as you are concerned.

Assume, now, that the recipient of your letter can overcome both these hurdles. He has still not reached the end of the trail. He must show that the damage was not 'too remote'. Take an example from an ordinary road traffic accident. Your employee caused it through careless driving? You are responsible, as if you yourself had been at the wheel, if the man was driving in the course of his employment. Therefore you would have to compensate anyone who suffered injury, loss or damage as a result – provided that this was foreseeable.

So the cost of repairing the other vehicle . . . or reimbursing the injured man for his lost wages . . . or damages in respect of his personal injuries – all these can be laid at your door.

But suppose, on the other hand, that the other driver missed an important appointment and hence a potentially profitable contract. That will be his misfortune. That damage was 'too remote'.

All this involves some very complicated legal consideration. If your letter-writing leads to the threat of legal action, the sooner you get to your solicitor, the better. Meanwhile, treat this chapter as a warning – and take care.

61

Liability for the Letters of Your Staff

Of course you do business on paper. You cannot write all your own letters, all of the time, can you? Even if you insist upon signing all your own mail, the odds are that chore-time comes at the end of the day, when your mind is weary and your soul longing for hearth or home, bed or bottle. So mistakes are made.

Or are you a chauffeur-driven executive, who signs his post in the back of the car? Then what if the driver lets his mind wander and negligently causes a collision?

Or maybe the man has dropped you at your door and is himself homeward bound when he causes the crash. Property is damaged. People are hurt.

Whether the employee's mistake is made in words or on wheels, his employer may not be the only sufferer. But who will be liable to pay? We look now, then, at the legal rules on vicarious liability – when the sins of the servant may be laid at the master's door.

The basic rule is simple. Every employer is liable to third parties in respect of damage caused by an employee within the scope of his employment. If you have the benefit of a man's work, then you must accept the burden of his mistakes. On the other hand, the mere fact that you employ a person does not mean that he is bound to you, every long hour of the day. He is entitled to go off 'on an independent frolic of his own'. And even when he does so improperly, he is outside the scope of his employment and the boss bears no responsibility for his misdeeds.

To take the most obvious example, your secretary may operate a typing bureau from her home. If she does so on her own account and in her own time, then she is responsible for her own negligence. You normally bear no liability.

Or maybe your driver causes a crash when off on an evening's gambol with his girl-friend. The fact that he happens to be in the company car will not fix liability upon the company.

Unfortunately, at this stage the law loses its clarity. The cases which reach court are borderline. The judge has to decide: was the negligent employee acting 'within the course of his employment' – or was he 'independently frolicking'?

An attendant at a petrol station was forbidden to smoke. He lit a cigarette and threw down a match. In the devasting explosion which resulted, property belonging to third parties was destroyed.

'He was not employed to smoke', argued his employers. 'Indeed, he was forbidden to do so.'

'He was employed to put petrol into tanks', said the court. 'At the time of the accident, that is precisely what he was doing – albeit in a thoroughly negligent, improper and forbidden manner.' His employers were liable.

So the test is *not:* 'Was the man doing that which was forbidden?', but rather: 'Was he about his master's business?'. By all means tell your employees what not to do and (if their misbehaviour is sufficiently serious) sack them if they disobey. But in so far as third parties are concerned, what matters is whether or not the employee was doing his job.

Or take the driver who goes off his route. Is he about his own business or that of his company or firm? Often, we have a baffling question of degree.

What of the employee who is guilty of skylarking? In one case, it was held that the 'fooling around' was done in the course of the man's employment, so his employers were liable for damage done. In another epic on similar facts, a court came to the opposite conclusion.

Suppose, then, that your secretary is guilty of a clerical error. Perhaps she leaves a nought off the price of goods offered. At the foot of the document we read: 'Dictated by Mr Smith but signed in his absence'. Poor, unfortunate Mr Smith – he should have been there.

The company will be bound by the offer just as it would if Mr Smith had signed it himself – or, for that matter, if it carried the company seal.

You are asked for a reference? You hand it over to your personnel manager for attention? Negligently, he provides the wrong information – and in breach of your instructions he omits to include a disclaimer of liability? The recipient of the missive suffers damage through relying upon the carelessly written words? Then it will be no answer to the claim to say: 'My man was guilty, not I'. His carelessness, committed in the course of his employment by you, is your own. In some ways, husband and wife are still regarded as one, in the eyes of the law – but master and man are united far more often, when it comes to the rules on vicarious liability.

62

Opening the Mail

A letter arrives at the office, shop or factory. It is addressed to a member of staff, care of the firm. You open it. It turns out to contain some very confidential information. 'Anything that comes to the firm is liable to be opened', you say. But is this right? What is the legal position?

If the letter is addressed to : James Smith, c/o Jones Ltd, then Mr Smith must expect to have it opened. The normal procedure in most businesses is for the mail to be opened centrally and then passed out to the appropriate departments or individuals for attention.

If an envelope is marked 'Personal' or 'Confidential', then the employer has no right to open it. Instead of coming to the employee in the course of his employment, it simply arrives at the place of employment. To open it then would be to interfere with Her Majesty's mail.

There is no reported decision on the point; no one seems to have seen fit to sue the boss for opening his letter. But when there is some indication that the employee is to receive the letter personally and/or confidentially, then it is an offence to open it for him.

Unhappily, the post is sometimes used for vicious purposes. These include the sending of letter and parcel bombs; of 'poison-pen' letters; and of pornographic literature.

Members of Parliament and others in public life who are vulnerable to the cowardly evil of letter bombs should take specific advice from appropriate police or security officials. Some organisations screen mail. But individuals at risk should not only themselves watch their mail with an eagle and a suspicious eye but they should instruct, reinstruct and remind their staff to do the same. Once again: the security people will tell you what to look out for and how. But if any letter or package appears suspicious, do not move it. Call the police.

Poison-pen or filth letters have an explosive unpleasantness of their own.

'I take it you are familiar with the termination clause in your contract of employment, Hopgood?'

Part 8

THE LAW IN LETTERS

Introduction

It is impossible in a book of this size to include all law likely to affect your letter-writing. Much of it, in any event, is indicated in (much larger) companion volumes. But here are some of the rules you are most likely to need to apply in your letters – in particular those affecting contracts in general and contracts of employment in particular.

Contracts

A contract is a bargain made between two or more people. It has a number of essential elements. First there must be an unconditional offer. Second: this offer must be unconditionally accepted. Third: there must be 'consideration'. Fourth: the required formalities of the law must be complied with – and writing may be one of these. Let us start with the writing.

Generally, no formalities are required for a contract to be binding. Most contracts are as complete and binding in law if they are made orally as if every term were written out in letters of gold. Exceptions: contracts of guarantee or for the transfer of an interest in land must be evidenced by some sufficient note or memorandum in writing, signed by the party to be charged. Contracts of hire purchase, of insurance and for the transfer of shares require writing. But a contract to buy goods may be made orally, so a telephone conversation is sufficient to wrap up the deal.

Where a deal has not been made or confirmed in writing, it may be difficult to prove its terms. One party may say that one term was agreed, the other something different.

So do confirm your agreements in writing, whenever you can. And do make a note or confirm anything important said to you by telephone. Remember: if a dispute follows and reaches court, you will be allowed to refer in the witness box to notes made at the time.

'What about the other essentials?' First, the offer. 'I offer to sell you X quantity of Y brand goods.' That is an offer. Simple? Not necessarily. It is, for instance, important to distinguish an offer from a mere 'invitation to treat'. If you advertise certain goods, you will not necessarily be bound to sell those goods, either at the advertised price or at all. Basically, the position is the same as when goods are on display in a shop window. They are not 'offered for sale', in the technical, legal sense. The public are merely invited to make an offer to buy them. That offer may either be accepted or refused; or a counter-offer may be made.

Second, the offer must be *unconditional*. If you say, 'I'll sell you these goods, provided that I've enough in stock', you can get out of the deal if you have not enough in stock. It is not an offer which is capable of immediate acceptance.

Third essential: *unconditional* acceptance. The offer must be accepted in its entirety. For instance, suppose that you offer to buy certain goods which you see advertised. You set out the price you are prepared to pay, the dates when you wish to have delivery and you leave no 'ifs' or 'buts'. The supplier writes back saying: 'Thank you for your letter. Your order is hereby accepted and we confirm that delivery will be made in accordance therewith.' The deal is done.

Now suppose the letter of acceptance contains terms and conditions inconsistent with yours printed at the bottom or on the back. In effect, the supplier is saying: 'We accept your offer – but subject to your agreeing to our terms and conditions as printed hereon'. This is not an *unconditional* acceptance. It is a 'counter-offer' which may be accepted or rejected by the potential buyer, as he sees fit.

Once you realise this, you take a further look at the terms and conditions on documents of this kind. Remember that if you do nothing about them and simply accept the goods, the chances are that the counter-offer will be the offer and your acceptance of the goods will be the acceptance. Hence, that acceptance will be subject to the supplier's terms and conditions. If you have agreed to a term which says that the suppliers shall not be bound to accept returns on faulty goods which are not reported to them within fourteen days of delivery, that will be your look-out.

'But what if the buyer never reads one of the terms in tiny type?' Too bad. Provided that it is legible, it is still one of the terms of the contract. If people do not choose to read contractual documents, that is their look-out.

'What if they couldn't have understood the terms, even if they had read them?' Then they should have asked a lawyer to explain them.

If the customer is a 'minor' (under the age of 18) or a person of unsound mind, then he may be able to avoid his obligations. People suffering from an incapacity – whether it be due to their youthfulness or their mental incapacity – have special protection under the law and will normally only be bound by their contracts if these are for 'necessaries' – that is, goods reasonably necessary to them at the time when they buy them, having regard to their 'station in life' and to their 'actual needs' at that time. Even if they are 'necessaries', only a reasonable price will have to be paid.

Generally, the terms of the contract – whether they are oral or printed – are part of the bargain. If the bargain is binding, those terms will be included in it, provided only that these were sufficiently brought to the attention of the contracting parties.

'Like the words on the back of the ticket, referring you to the company's regulations?'

Precisely. But to return to 'acceptance'. Like an offer, an acceptance (if it is to conclude the bargain) must be unconditional. If, for instance, the buyer says: 'I accept your offer of these goods, subject to approval by my directors', then there would be no deal until the directors had given their approval and this fact was communicated to his suppplier.

Now comes the third essential: 'consideration'. This, in English law, simply means some *quid pro quo* – some return for the value or promise given. 'In consideration of our paying you £ . . . , you agree to supply me with Y thousand of the goods advertised.' The consideration 'moving' in one direction is the promise to pay the specified sum. The consideration 'moving' in the other direction is the promise to supply the goods concerned in return for that sum.

'But when is there no consideration?' Suppose you are a sales manager and you write to a special customer: 'I'll send you a crate of whisky for Christmas . . .'. Unless the giving of the whisky was in return for a promise to buy goods, he can do nothing if you never send the drink. It was a gratuitous promise and you had given nothing in return.

Or suppose that a customer writes to you: 'I'd be very much obliged to you if you'd hold those goods for me'.

'With pleasure, Sir', you reply. But in fact you sell them to someone else who offers a higher price and when your original customer asks for them, he finds that they no longer exist. Bad luck. There was no 'consideration' for you holding them, and therefore no binding contract. You are in luck.

'The customer should have put down a deposit, I suppose . . .'. Correct. He would then have been saying, 'In consideration of my giving you this deposit, you agree to hold the goods at our disposal for the specified period'. If you had accepted his money, you would have been bound to give the customer the option on the goods concerned for the period agreed.

Conversely (the deposit being an 'earnest of good faith' on the customer's part), if he had failed to exercise the option and to take up the goods, you would have been entitled to keep the deposit. As usual, you *could* have made some agreement to the contrary. You could, for instance, have agreed to give credit in the same sum as the deposit, if your customer decided to opt not to purchase . . .

If a buyer allows one of his servants to place an order on his behalf, then he is as bound by that order as if he had given it himself. This must be so or the business world would halt. A company has no existence in human form. Someone must act for it. Even individuals cannot do everything for themselves. If you give someone your authority to contract on your behalf, then you will not be able to avoid the contracts made by that person pursuant to that authority.

'But suppose that the person had no authority . . . can the principal then refuse to accept the arrangement made?' That depends. He can do so if the agent had neither his actual nor his 'apparent' authority. Otherwise he is almost certainly bound.

If you 'hold someone out' as having your authority to act on your behalf (if, in legal terms, you give him your 'ostensible' authority) then you are, in effect, saying to other people: 'This man is my agent, entitled to contract on my behalf'. If someone relies upon this statement and as a result makes a bargain with you, then you will be bound by that bargain. You must not 'hold out' people as having authority which they do not in fact possess. If you do, you cannot expect the law to free you from deals made as a result.

Finally, the contract must not be 'too vague to be enforceable'. The law will not make contracts for business people who do not bother to do so for themselves. So sometimes it is possible to avoid a contract if it can be shown that any of the essential elements of that contract are missing.

For example, suppose that your customers had agreed to buy goods. The delivery date was fixed and the goods themselves were decided upon. But you left the price unfixed. Alternatively, suppose that the price was fixed but that the quantity to be taken was not. In either case, one of the most essential terms of the deal was missing. The contract would be too vague to be enforced.

To sum up: if a person of full capacity makes an unconditional offer which is unconditionally accepted by some other person of full capacity and the terms of the contract are adequately set out and agreed between them – and provided that there is 'consideration' – the contract is complete. Where an agent makes the contract on behalf of his principal, it rarely matters whether that agent had the actual authority of the principal to contract on his behalf. It is enough if the agent had his principal's apparent authority to do so. And writing is only necessary in exceptional cases.

64

Restraint Clauses

When an employee changes his job, his greatest asset is his own knowledge and know-how, skill and experience. But how much of this is he entitled to use for the benefit of his new organisation? If you leave your company, will it be able to prevent you from working for a competitor – or on your own account? The answers entirely depend upon whether or not there is a valid, binding restraint clause in your contract of employment.

The law does its best to see that everyone is free to use all his talents and abilities to his own best advantage. It insists that a person be entitled to earn a living, to win promotion, to improve his prospects. A man's knowledge is part of himself. He cannot leave it behind when he moves on to other work. So, in general, he is free to use it either for his new employers or, if he decides to strike out on his own, for himself.

This does not mean that you may use secret information belonging to your ex-employers. If, for instance, your company operates a particular confidential process, you will not be entitled to abuse that confidence when you leave your post. But subject to this proviso, you may usually make free use of all that you have learned in the company's service.

Equally, you are not expected to lose your friends, acquaintances or contacts, simply because you change your employer. If you are employed as a director by a new company, they do not just get you and your experience. They also acquire your status, your prestige, your contracts. Even if you do not move, the fact that your present company knows that you could do so and that you would then be able to use your contacts for others is one of the best incentives for seeing that you are properly paid for your present work.

If you do move on, you are usually able to contact suppliers or customers who do business with your previous company. But there is one major limitation. You are not entitled to take with you any mailing lists or other documents which belong to your previous employers. If you do so, then the court may grant an injunction restraining you from making use of these documents and ordering you to return them to your previous employers.

All this only applies in the absence of some enforceable agreement to the contrary. If there is a valid, binding restraint clause in a contract of service, the company may be able to prevent the employee from competing against it when he leaves. But as such a clause is 'in restraint of trade', putting as it does a limit on the employee's freedom, it is frowned upon by the law and is *prima facie* void as 'contrary to public policy'.

A 'restraint clause' will only be enforced if it is 'reasonable' from everyone's point of view. It must not be so broad in extent that the employee cannot make a living. It must not be more extensive than is reasonably necessary for the proper protection of the employer's business. And it must not be unreasonable from the viewpoint of the public.

It is often extremely difficult to know whether a particular clause is likely to be upheld. No layman can ever know whether a restraint clause is or is not likely to be enforceable. So I emphasise again – these terms, if they are to be of any use at all, should be drafted by lawyers, skilled in the art. They will know from their own experience what terms courts allow and what they disallow.

Examples? A covenant not to solicit customers will be void if it extends to people who became customers after the service terminated. A company will only be entitled to protection in respect of that part of the business in which the employee was actually engaged. A covenant preventing a person from carrying on any business is utterly void. So is one intended to protect not merely the business of the company itself but also that of a subsidiary or associated company in which the employee did not serve.

Agree not to solicit people who were customers of the company while you were still employed and this restraint will normally be valid, even if it is unrestricted as to time or space. But generally, if the restraint is over too wide an area or for too long a time, it will be a dead letter.

To find out whether a particular clause is likely to be enforceable, you must consult a lawyer. Remember that the court is most unlikely to cut down the clause to reasonable size. Like every egg except that of the famous curate, it is either all good or all bad. In legal terms, it is rarely 'severable'. If it is unreasonable, it is normally useless.

So if you are dealing with a restraint clause in your own contract of service, you should either ensure that it is omitted altogether or that it is so wide as to be unenforceable. Otherwise, you must reckon to be bound by it. And if you are dealing with restraint clauses in the contracts of employees, sweet reason must rule supreme! Unreasonable clauses are not worth the paper they are written on.

65

Contracts of Employment

A contract of employment is an agreement between employer and employee under which the employee agrees to serve and the employer to employ, on the terms stated. A contract of employment does not have to be in writing to be binding in law. But thanks to *The Employment Protection (Consolidation) Act 1978*, the employee must be given written particulars of its most important terms within 13 weeks of the commencement of his employment or within four weeks of any variation.

The written statement which may be contained in one or more letters or other documents must identify the parties (especially important if the employer is a company which is part of a group). It must specify the date when the employment began and state whether or not the employment is continuous with any previous employment (if so, then when did that employment begin?). It must state the employee's job title. And it must give the following particulars of the terms of employment as at a specified date not more than one week before the statement is given:

1   The scale or rate of remuneration, or the method of calculating remuneration.
2   The intervals at which remuneration is paid (that is, whether weekly or monthly or by some other period).
3   Any terms and conditions relating to hours of work (including any terms and conditions relating to normal working hours).
4   Any terms and conditions relating to:
    a   Holidays and holiday pay (including the manner in which holiday entitlement is arrived at, especially when the employment comes to an end);
    b   Incapacity for work due to sickness or injury, including any provisions for sick pay;
    c   Pensions and pension schemes.
5   The length of notice which the employee is obliged to give and entitled to receive to determine his contract of employment.
6   To whom the employee may turn if he has a grievance or a query regarding disciplinary procedures – and either details of both grievance and disciplinary procedures or where these may be easily found.

The particulars need not be in any set form and may (and generally should) include other terms not required by law, such as:

a   Clauses giving employers the right to search employees or their property.
b   Restraint clauses (see Chapter 64).
c   Clauses warning employees that breaches of the employer's health and safety rules may lead to dismissal.

An employee is (generally, and in broad terms) only entitled by law to written particulars if he has been employed for 13 weeks. Like employees entitled to unfair dismissal protection and redundancy pay, he must normally work at least 16 hours a week or 8 hours after 5 years' continuous service.

66

Wrongful Dismissal and Unfair Dismissal

Unless an employee has earned himself the summary sack – by some dreadful misconduct which 'repudiates' (or smashes) the contract – he is normally entitled to his proper notice. This is:

1   Such period as has been agreed (and the agreement should be set out in writing – see Chapter 65).
2   In the absence of agreement, he is entitled to reasonable notice; and in any event –
3   Not less than the statutory minimum, which now is seven days after four weeks' service; two weeks after two years, three weeks after three years; and so on up to 12 weeks after 12 years.

An employee who is not given his proper notice is dismissed 'wrongfully' and may claim damages from a civil court (County Court or High Court, depending on the amount involved).

An employee may be dismissed 'unfairly', whether or not he is given his notice. Exceptions include: those who have reached normal retiring age (or 65 for men, 60 for women); those who do not 'normally work' 16 hours a week or 8 hours after five years' continuous service; those not employed for the minimum one year (two years for small firms); and those based outside the UK.

Claims for compensation for unfair dismissal go to industrial tribunals. Successful claimants may now get as much as £18,980, made up as follows:

a   Compensatory award – up to £7,500 to compensate the claimant for loss of earnings and fringe benefits (for up to two years).
b   Basic award – up to £4,200 (current maximum lost redundancy entitlement).
c   Additional award – up to £7,280 where the employer has unreasonably failed to comply with an order for the reinstatement of the employee in his job.

In practice, claims for unfair dismissal are far more likely and common than those for wrongful dismissal. Tribunals are full of them. The stakes are high and the perils are many. If you are likely to get involved in a hearing, take legal advice. If you are acting personally, you will not get legal aid to enable you to be represented by solicitor or counsel at the hearing, but you may well qualify for legal advice at little or no cost. Although the lawyer will not be able to help you to present your case, he will assist you to prepare it. Preparation includes, of course, the writing of the appropriate letters.

67

If You Give No Notice

You are offered a more lucrative post, provided that you leave at once. Alternatively, you have just about had enough of your present company and can stand it no longer. So you decide to leave without giving proper notice. What can the law do about it? Suppose that, as a result, the company suffers a severe loss of business. Would it have any remedy against you?

Can you be forced to return to your employers, to serve out the period of notice? Can they get an injunction against you to prevent you from working for anyone else during the period of notice? Alternatively, what about suing you for damages? After all, even if the company thinks that you are not really worth suing, it will not want other executives to think that contracts of service can be flaunted without fear of the consequences.

Normally, sauce for the goose is sauce for the gander also. A breach of contract leads to legal consequences whether the contract-breaker happens to be master or servant, supplier or customer, solicitor or client, but the employer whose employee has left without giving proper notice has, in the main, rights in theory only.

An injunction is an order of the court forbidding or restraining a particular kind of behaviour, or (in the case of a so-called 'mandatory injunction') requiring that a certain thing be done in order that an unlawful state of affairs be terminated.

If courts wish to force employees to return to their employers to serve out their periods of notice, the remedy they could give would be an injuction. This could either restrain the ex-employee from working for others during his period of notice, or order him to return to his employers until his contractual service was properly concluded.

But courts do their best not to impose restrictions on people's freedom to earn their living. Other than in the most exceptional circumstances (such as where there is a valid contract in restraint of trade) courts will not forbid employees from working for particular employers. So the first type of injunction is not available to the innocent employer whose employee has given no notice.

Equally, courts do their best not to make orders which they cannot ensure are obeyed and which will only lead to probable trouble. If they were to require that an employee return to his company, to work out a period of notice, they could certainly see that he physically turned up. But the inevitable result would be that the employee's heart would not be in the job, his company would complain that he was not doing that job properly, and the parties would be back in court. Judges cannot stand over the shoulders of the contract-breaking staff, and as they can only bring the horse to water and do nothing to see that he actually drinks, no such order will be made in the first place. Anyway, once again, to do so would mean infringing an employee's liberty to sell the only product which he usually has to offer – his own labour.

That leaves damages. In theory, a master is certainly entitled to damages if his employee leaves without giving proper notice, but whereas the employee can prove his financial loss to the last penny, the employer can seldom prove the amount of money he has lost through the breach of contract. In legal jargon, he cannot 'quantify his damage'. He cannot express it in 'liquidated terms'. And where damages of this kind cannot be quantified, they cannot be recovered.

Take the ordinary case. A senior member of staff does not return from holiday. As a result one of the company's departments is thrown into chaos. All sorts of people have to do extra work and the company may be certain that it has lost both goodwill and business. But what is the amount of such loss?

'Last year in the same month we made £X', you say. 'This year we made £X minus £Y. We attribute the difference to the absence of Mr Z, before a replacement had been obtained for him.'

That sounds fine, but it will not hold water. After all, there are dozens of other reasons why profits over the period concerned may have gone down. Trade advances and recedes. Demand for a product fluctuates. Other staff may fall ill. One customer may have been lost for entirely different reasons. In fact, it is seldom possible to lay any loss of this kind at the door of a departed employee.

'What about the extra hours which other employees had to work?' No good. Only if they had received extra pay as a result could it be shown that a specific financial loss was attributable to the absence. In fact, about the only damages which can generally be recovered from an employee who leaves without notice are the costs involved in training his replacement. And they are a drop in the bucket and no real compensation for the unfortunate boss.

The answer, then, is that while master and servant have, in theory, identical rights arising out of identical breaches of contract, in practice this is one occasion when an employee is one up on the boss. And that makes up for many times when he is several down.

'*I see you've asked for one or two other offences to be taken into account . . .*'.

Part 9

LETTERS – AND LITIGATION

Introduction

Two businessmen had operated a successful partnership for years. They fell out and sued each other. Vigorous efforts were made to settle the case and by the time it arrived at court, the lawyers had agreed on everything except who was to pay the legal costs.

'Tell you what', said Jones to his solicitor. 'I'll have a word with old Williams and see whether we can't come to some arrangement.'

'A good idea', said his lawyer. Jones collared Williams and they went off into a corner. Five minutes later they were back, smiling. 'We're agreed', they said, in chorus.

'But what about the costs?', queried the lawyers.

'We're agreed on that, too', Jones replied. 'He's not going to pay his and I'm not going to pay mine!'

That is what they thought.

In fact, law costs – plenty. If your letter-writing is defective, your contracts unclear, your deals in dispute, then you are likely to run into very heavy expense indeed. So here are some basic hints and rules on letters and litigation.

Letters Before Action – and When Should You Sue?

Almost any letter may find its way into a bundle of correspondence, placed before a court. If you are likely to be on the winning side, then if you have sufficient foresight, you may well design your letter for that specific purpose. If you are wise, you will not sue unless you really have to.

'When should I sue?', you ask. 'Is it worth chasing the company's debtors to court? Or is that simply throwing good money after bad? Should I get a solicitor to chase up my accounts? Or am I better off to have another go myself? How far can the law help the businessman to get in his money – before his own cheques begin to bounce?'

A man asked his lawyer these questions. Here is what he was told:

'If your demands for payment are ignored . . . your invoices torn up . . . your statements added to the waste pile . . . then the sooner you put the case into the hands of your lawyer, the better. It's incredible how many poor payers leap into action when they receive solicitors' "letters before action". They don't mind ignoring colleagues in the trade, but they don't like to tangle with the law.'

'How much would it cost to have you write?', inquired the careful client.

'A pound or two. Worth every penny.'

'If that doesn't work?'

The lawyer smiled. 'Then every case must be considered on its own facts', he said. 'First, can the debtor be easily found? If he can't and if you have to pay professional process servers to deliver your writ, then, if the amount involved isn't large, you'd best forget it. Then again, is he a man of straw? It's no use getting a judgement against a penniless defendant. You can't eat moral satisfaction.'

'I thought that the courts could make judgement debtors pay by instalments . . .'

'So they can. You get an order for £1 a month . . . it's not complied with . . . you send a lawyer to question the debtor in court . . . the debtor gets the order reduced . . . and so on. It costs you more to chase your debt than it would have done to write it off. Of course, lots of debtors pretend to be broke – in which case bankruptcy petitions, threats of liquidation proceedings, garnishee orders and such-like legal thumbscrews, often force the unwilling debtor to liquidate those hidden securities, and convince him that the rainy day has arrived.'

'Suppose that you know where the debtor is and he has got money. What then?'

'Then you must ask, has he a defence to your claim? Would he convince the court that the goods were substandard or not up to sample, the work delivered too late, the machinery defective . . . ? After all, it's not much good prosecuting a claim that you're going to lose, is it?'

'Not unless you can get a good settlement.'

'I agree. Well, anyway, there's not much to lose by issuing a writ or a summons. If the claim does not exceed £5,000, you bring your action in the County Court. If it's for a higher amount, then it's the High Court for you.* In either case, you'll probably find that the little piece of paper from the court will shake your debtor into activity. The vast majority of cases that are started never reach trial – unhappily for the legal profession! Where a solicitor's letter fails, writs and summonses often succeed.'

*Or their Scottish equivalents.

'How much will all this cost?'

'A few pounds. And if this doesn't bring results, you can always quit, even at that stage.'

'How much will a case cost if it does get to trial?'

'£100–5,000 . . . It's impossible to tell. Everything depends upon its complication . . . , how long it will last . . . , how high-powered the counsel we brief. But one thing I warn you: even if you win, you'll not get all the legal costs back from the other side. The costs will be "taxed" (that is, assessed) by an officer of the court, and he'll divide them, generally speaking, into three groups. First, there'll be "party and party" costs, necessarily incurred for the doing of justice and usually paid by the losing litigant. Then come the "solicitor and client" – or "common fund" – costs, properly incurred, but not absolutely essential and therefore not to be laid at the loser's door. Finally, there are those which the court feels were really unnecessary and the lawyer can forget them altogether. They'll be struck off his bill.'

'And do "solicitor and client" costs usually amount to much?'

'Again, it all depends. So write your letters . . . consult your solicitor . . . get him to write . . . and even issue your writ or your summons. But before you sue, make quite sure that you really want to. Litigation is a very expensive luxury. It should be kept as a very last resort.'

69

Litigants, Lawyers and Courts of Law

If you are forced into litigation, either as plaintiff, defendant or accused, what must you expect? How can you best prepare yourself for battle? Need you – and should you – employ solicitor or counsel?

Whether you are appearing in a civil or in a criminal court, the essence of British procedure is that each side presents its case as effectively as possible and the court – be it a judge, jury, stipendiary (paid) magistrate or a Bench of lay (unpaid) justices – will then decide upon the winner.

The prosecution in a criminal court must normally prove its case 'beyond all reasonable doubt'. If there is any real doubt as to the defendant's guilt, he is entitled to the benefit of it. There are exceptions – under the Health and Safety at Work Act, for instance, if the defendant agrees that there was an unsafe practice but says that he took all reasonably practicable steps to deal with it, then the burden of proving innocence rests on him.

In a civil action, the judge decides 'on the balance of probabilities'. The court must make up its mind one way or the other. It must say whether, on balance, it accepts the case for the plaintiff or that for the defendant. An industrial tribunal will look at all the circumstances of the case, including the 'size and administrative resources' of the employer's business, before deciding whether the dismissal was – on balance – 'fair' or 'unfair'.

Naturally, the presentation of a case matters. There are some court actions which so obviously go one way or the other that even the most skilled advocate with the finest training and experience cannot alter the outcome. But most cases are not so simple. It matters how they are presented to a court.

There are two main kinds of evidence, oral and documentary. Witnesses testify as to their recollection of what happened. Even the most honest of witnesses may be mistaken. So where there are documents, these are vitally important. As a witty judge remarked: 'As time goes on, memory fades, but recollection improves!'.

The most common documents are letters. If you have a dispute with a supplier or a customer, a contractor or an employee (or with anyone else, for that matter) make sure that anything which goes into writing sets out your position accurately. Equally, the majority of those convicted by our criminal courts are found guilty on their own admissions or on the basis of statements they have themselves given to the police. It is far better to exercise your legal right to say nothing than to make any statement which you may later regret. Silence is golden.

If in doubt about the statement you propose giving to the police or a letter which you wish to write about a dispute, then is the time to go to your solicitor. Begrudge a lawyer's fee at that stage and the odds are that you will have to pay him tenfold later on. Litigation should be nipped in the bud . . . Cases should be prepared from their inception . . . . It is useless to destroy your own case and then to expect a lawyer to put it together again for you. Only a fool would put up a building first and then call in an architect. Do not invite your lawyer to take on a case after you have lost it.

Once you get to court, the odds are that you ought to be represented. 'A man who is his own lawyer has a fool for a client', goes the old saying. And if you already have a lawyer, use him. 'It's no good keeping a dog and doing the barking yourself . . .' Only in industrial tribunals are you generally wise to represent yourself.

If you operate your business through a company, then you have no right of audience other than by solicitor or counsel. A solicitor is entitled to appear in any lower court – Magistrates' Court, County Court, or tribunal. A barrister has the right of audience in any court of the land, right up to the House of Lords. A company, being a fictitious entity with no real human life, has no right of audience anywhere. It must appear by its legal representative.

The lowest criminal courts are the Magistrates' Courts and the vast bulk of criminal work is done by them. More serious cases are dealt with by the Crown Court or (in the case of appeals) by a Divisional Court of the Queen's Bench Division or by the Court of Appeal (Criminal Division). On matters of great public importance, the House of Lords may be called upon to give its ruling.

The High Court is divided into three divisions. The Queen's Bench Division deals with 'common law' cases – as opposed to those cases which were, on the whole, within the prerogative of the old, Lord Chancellor's Courts, now in the Chancery Division. Company and partnership cases, matters involving trusts and often land – these are the usual sort of Chancery actions.

The jurisdiction of the Family Division comprises matrimonial causes, matrimonal property, children and non-contentious probate (wills and intestacy) work.

Industrial tribunals deal with redundancy, unfair dismissal, equal pay and most other disputes involving employment. The chairman of a tribunal is legally qualified; he sits with two colleagues – generally, one with experience of management and the other of the shop floor; and they mete out swift, inexpensive justice.

So there is your guide to the courts and tribunals in a nutshell.

70

Letters in Dispute

The more serious or costly the dispute, the more vital the correspondence is likely to prove – and the more weighty its probative value. So the courts have evolved a system to ensure that most correspondence, material to an action, is revealed to the other side (if they do not already possess it) and produced for the court's inspection. This process is called 'discovery of documents'.

In any legal action, the parties must set out their contentions in so-called 'pleadings'. In the High Court (which deals, in general, with claims over £5,000), the plaintiff's 'cause of action' is pleaded in a 'Statement of Claim'. Normally, in a case of any complication, this will be drafted by Counsel. Otherwise, a solicitor will have done it.

Next, the defendant puts his answer into a 'Defence'. This may include a 'Counterclaim'. The plaintiff will then file his 'Reply' and 'Defence to Counterclaim'.

In the County Court, an action starts with a 'Particulars of Claim' – and this, in its turn, is succeeded by a Defence (with or without Counterclaim) and a Reply.

If any of the 'pleadings' happens to be obscure or not to set out the case in sufficient detail, 'Further and Better Particulars' may be sought by the other party. 'Tell us more', he says. If the litigant has not declared his case adequately, he will now have to do so – if necessary as a result of a court order.

The object of the exercise, then, is to enable the trial judge to have the contentions of both sides spread out before him, so that (on the basis of the evidence, and the law) he may decide the matter, one way or the other.

Now, if any document is referred to in a pleading, the other party is entitled to a copy of it. If, for instance, your claim rests upon a letter or an invoice, or upon written particulars of a contract of employment, the other party may demand a copy – and upon payment of the appropriate copying charges (if any) he is entitled to get one.

Moreover, where a pleading does not specifically rely upon a document, but there may be some relevant (or 'material') letter, plan, map, order form or what-have-you, upon which the party intends to rely, the other litigant may demand that the document be 'identified'.

Once 'the pleadings are closed' – the contentions of the parties clearly set out on paper – the time has come for each to reveal the documents relevant to the proceedings, which are or have been in his possession. 'Discovery' will take place of all material documents, and these must then be made available for 'inspection'. A litigant is not allowed to keep some useful document up his sleeve and to produce it with a flourish at the hearing, preferably whilst cross-examining a star witness on the other side. He must reveal it beforehand.

To make sure that he does so, a formal list of documents has to be prepared and presented. Sometimes, the list will be supported by an affidavit in which the litigant swears that these are all the relevant documents which are or have been in his possession. Sometimes, instead of a list, the documents will be set out as part of an affidavit.

Not all relevant documents must be shown to the other side. Some are 'privileged'. For instance, any correspondence which you may have with your own solicitor will be privileged. Nor will you have to produce an Advice given to you by your own Counsel. But letters which passed between the parties and which were not written 'without prejudice' (see Chapter 71) will have to be revealed, even if these happen to go dead against your case.

So that explains, does it not, precisely why the art of letter-writing is such an important adjunct to successful litigation. Careless letters cost cases. To be well prepared may be worth a fortune. So mind how you write. Your letter may one day be read out in court. Alternatively, it may win your case long before it reaches trial – and that, of course, is by far the best sort of legal victory.

71

'Without Prejudice'

What is the effect of putting 'without prejudice' at the top of your letters? If the businessman enters into negotiations which (inevitably) involve concessions on his part, can these be thrown back into his teeth, if the negotiations fail and the case gets to court? How far is it safe to make admissions in correspondence, if you add the magic words 'without prejudice' at the top of the letter?

The answers were given in the notable case of *Tomlin* v. *Standard Telephones & Cables Ltd.*

The facts were fairly typical. Mr Tomlin was injured at work and sued his employers. Negotiations followed between his solicitors and his employers' insurers. Eventually, the insurers made an offer which was refused. Mr Tomlin pressed forward with his action. He also alleged that an agreement had been arrived at during the negotiations that he was entitled to be compensated on the basis of fifty per cent liability, although it was conceded that the *amount* of damages was left in the air.

Was the correspondence between the parties admissible? All the letters that mattered had been marked 'without prejudice'. Eventually, by a majority of two to one, the Court of Appeal decided that, in the circumstances, the letters could be looked at by the court.

The effect of 'without prejudice' letters was laid down by a judge, many years ago. He said this: 'I think they mean "without prejudice" to the position of the writer of the letter if the terms he proposes *are not* accepted. If the terms proposed in the letter are accepted a complete contract is established, and the letter, although written "without prejudice", operates to alter the old state of things and to establish a new one.'

So 'not only is the court entitled to look at the letters in this case', said Lord Justice Danckwerts, 'although they were described as "without prejudice", it is quite possible (and, in fact, the intention of the parties was) that there was a binding agreement contained in their correspondence.'

In other words, once 'without prejudice' negotiations are alleged to have reached fruition, the court must be entitled to look at the letters to see whether that allegation is well founded. As Sir Gordon Willmer put it: 'It is no objection that the agreement is contained in letters which are headed "without prejudice".' If you make an agreement, then you cannot say: 'It was only made in the course of negotiations'. If the negotiations had failed, then the court would be entitled to know that there were in fact attempts at settlement, but the letters themselves would remain privileged. Once an agreement is reached, the court must be entitled to look at the letters in which it is contained. And if the parties cannot agree as to whether or not the letters contained a binding agreement, the court must examine them, if it is to decide.

Mr Justice Ormrod dissented. But his observations are helpful nonetheless. He said: 'The court will protect, and ought to protect so far as it can, in the public interest, "without prejudice" negotiations because they are very helpful to the disposal of claims without the necessity for litigating in court. Therefore, nothing should be done to make more difficult or more hazardous negotiations under the umbrella of "without prejudice".

'I am well aware that letters get headed "without prejudice" in the most absurd circumstances, but the letters in the present case are not so headed unnecessarily or meaninglessly. They are plainly "without prejudice" letters. Therefore the Court should be very slow to lift the umbrella of "without prejudice" unless the case is absolutely plain.'

The judge looked at the correspondence, but decided that the case was not 'absolutely plain'.

Anyway, the principle is now clear enough. By all means mark your letters 'without prejudice', so as to ensure that if no agreement is reached, your position will not be prejudiced through any admissions or confessions that you may have made. But once there is an agreement resulting from the negotiations, they cease to be 'without prejudice'. They are open for all the world to see.

Another case when letters (but not their contents) may be considered is where there is a question of unreasonable delay. In several recent cases, plaintiffs have been driven out of court because they did not see fit to pursue their claims with sufficient vigour. Cases are nowadays 'dismissed for want of prosecution' much more readily than ever before. On the other hand, it would be quite wrong for claims to be dismissed through delay where the object of the exercise was to attempt to avoid court battle through 'without prejudice' parleys. So by all means allow or encourage your solicitors to haggle. But if they delay when negotiations have ceased, then harry and nag them.

Still, the contents of 'without prejudice' letters are only admissible where an offer contained in them has been accepted. So a court will not be allowed to see them merely where they contain admissions or acknowledgements of a debt, where it is alleged that the debt has become 'statute barred'. If the six-year period has passed since the debt was incurred or acknowledged in writing, the fact that there were intervening negotiations will not revive it.

Again, if you want to keep your rights under *The Landlord and Tenant Act 1954,* you must serve your notices and if necessary make application to the court within the period specified. If you are kept haggling until that date has passed, your rights will be lost. And whether the negotiations were oral or in writing, provided that they were 'without prejudice', your landlord's position will remain unaffected – unless, of course, you can prove you actually reached an agreement.

The privilege which the law gives to 'without prejudice' letters may be 'waived' by the consent of both parties to the negotiations. If both agree that the court ought to see the letters, then so be it. If the writer of the letter wishes to waive the privilege, there are some lawyers who think that he can do so. Most believe that without the consent of both parties or agreement which becomes binding upon them, the position of neither party may be improved or worsened through their revealing to the court words (oral or written) intended to have been used 'without prejudice' only.

So while Tomlin's case shows the limits on the doctrine, the basic principle remains unaffected. Put your negotiations under the umbrella of 'without prejudice' letters, and if agreement escapes you, the chances are that the letters will remain hidden from the judical eye, now and for ever more.

72

Proof of Posting

'We never received your letter', you write.

'Too bad', answers your supplier (or customer or other correspondent). 'We can prove that we posted it; you will be presumed by law to have received it; so the offer you originally made was validly accepted by us – and you had no right to sell the goods elsewhere.'

'Rubbish', you answer. But are you right? And anyway, how could your correspondent prove that he actually posted the letter? If a contract is made by post (and most of them are), is it firm and binding when a letter of acceptance is posted or when it is received? At what stage can you (or your correspondent) still cry off?

Recent cases decided that where a contract is entered into wholly or partly by correspondence, and where an offer is made by letter, the deal is done as soon as a 'properly addressed letter containing the acceptance is posted'. Provided that the 'offeree' accepts unconditionally and within the time specified in the correspondence, the 'offeror' cannot clamber out of his obligations by alleging that he never received the letter.

So proof of posting becomes important. At best, the sender has taken the trouble to call in at the Post Office and has obtained a receipt for the letter. Alternatively, he may have sent it registered. 'Recorded delivery' will show despatch and delivery with equal certainty.

'That's all very well', you say, 'in theory. But the vast majority of commercial correspondence is posted in the ordinary way, without any sort of post office record. What then?'

Then you should have a proper posting book, in which your clerk or office junior notes down the addressee of each letter, before it is stamped or franked. Production of the book is not absolute proof. After all, the employee may have dropped the post down the drain whilst on the way to the letter-box. But there will be a presumption of posting which the addressee will find very difficult to rebut.

'The posting of a letter', says the law, 'may be proved by the person who posted it, or by showing facts from which posting may be presumed.' Hence 'evidence of posting may be given by proving that a letter was delivered to a clerk who in the ordinary course of business would have posted it.' Alternatively, it could be shown that the letter was put into a box which is normally cleared by the postman.

Again, if a letter is properly dated, that date will be taken as evidence of the date upon which it was written or dictated. In fact, evidence may show that dictation occurred a day or more before. The postmark on the envelope is splendid evidence as to the time and place of posting. Unfortunately, the recipient is likely to toss that envelope into the nearest waste-paper basket.

It follows that it is worth the while of every businessmen to work out a sensible system for the recording of letters posted. And because these rules apply both ways, the stamping of a date of receipt on all incoming post is a very sensible precaution.

Note   The rules are rather different where acceptance of an offer is by telex. Two cases, one most recently in the House of Lords – *Brinkibon* v. *Stahag* (1982) – have established that the same general rule applicable to instantaneous communication also applies to telex.

Where an offer is accepted by telex, the time of acceptance is when the telex is sent and the place of acceptance will normally be where the telex is received and read and not (as in the case of a letter) the place from which it is sent.

'That will be the last letter for today Miss Wilkins . . . .'

Part 10

APPENDICES

Post Office Services

Introduction

You may, of course, send your letter or card by hand. But the odds are that (for better or for worse) you will use the services provided by the Post Office. And that use could be a great deal better, if you knew more about it.

Here, then, is a summary of the services offered by the Post Office (with my thanks to them, for their co-operation). The descriptions are, of necessity, brief and you are advised to consult the *Post Office Guide* for full details. You may regard some of the items as a checklist, worth a few moments of your time to ensure that you are making the best of the services which you know to exist. But you will also find some lesser-known services which may well save you a good deal of time, aggravation, worry – and expense – and hence contribute towards your commercially successful letter-writing.

Letters

The system of first- and second-class postal services for inland letters is well established and all businessmen are familiar with it. We do not include details of rates for letters here since these have been more or less regularly increased and remain liable to change. Two points are, however, worth noting here. First, inland rates apply to letters from the UK to the Isle of Man, the Channel Islands and the Irish Republic. Second, the maximum admissible weight for a second-class letter is 750 g – so really heavy letters are often sent much more economically by parcel post.

Discounts on postage for pre-sorted second-class letters

Bulk rebates Postage must be pre-paid at the appropriate letter rate for mail posted in bulk; but, subject to certain conditions, a bulk mailing pre-sorted by the poster into post towns and counties may attract rebate of postage on the following scale on second-class letters posted for delivery in the UK. Rebates are not available for bulk postings from the UK to the Channel Islands, the Isle of Man or the Irish Republic.

Number of letters	Amount of rebate
4,250(minimum) –4,999	Postage paid on all letters in excess of 4,250
5,000–23,529	15% of the postage paid on all letters
23,530–24,999	Postage paid on all letters in excess of 20,000
25,000–96,875	20% of the postage paid on all letters
96,876–99,999	Postage paid on all letters in excess of 77,500
100,000–241,935	22½% of the postage paid on all letters
241,936–249,999	Postage paid on all letters in excess of 187,500
250,000–933,333	25% of the postage paid on all letters
933,334–999,999	Postage paid on all letters in excess of 700,000
One million or more	30% of the postage paid on all letters

The rebate is allowed after the letters have been posted and checked. Delivery of rebate items will usually be completed within seven working days (excluding weekends and public holidays) after posting.

Second-class discounts   Similarly, posters who pre-sort mailings into post towns and counties, but require normal second-class delivery, will be allowed a discount of 12 per cent of the postage due on items pre-sorted to post towns and 7 per cent of the postage due on items pre-sorted to counties. In both cases the discount will be reduced by 2 per cent if items are not fully postcoded. Mailings should usually be of at least 5,000 identical second-class letters to qualify.

Discounts on postage for first-class letters

Discounts are also available for bulk postings of first-class mail. Savings of 12 per cent are possible for postings of 5,000 letters or more under contract.

Receipts

A receipt for a bulk posting pre-paid in stamps will be supplied free on request.

Incentive discount for growth

Posters spending more than £20,000 per year on inland letter postage may qualify for a discount on any real value year-on-year increase in that expenditure. The discount is 2 per cent of every 1 per cent of increased expenditure, up to a maximum of 20 per cent for a 10 per cent increase or more. A poster must have achieved at least a 3 per cent real value increase before the discount is applicable.

Price protection

Direct mail deposit system   A contractual facility for direct mail advertisers. An advertiser who wishes to protect a mailing against the possibility of a postal tariff change occurring before the posting date planned for that mailing may do so by depositing with the Post Office 25 per cent of the postage due on that mailing, calculated at the rates current at the time the deposit is lodged. The deposit may be made up to six months in advance of the mailing date.

A mailing to be protected must be of at least 5,000 identical items containing advertising material only, and full details of the size, nature and timing of the mailing will be required. (A Direct Mail Deposit may not be used to protect a mailing against a proposed tariff increase that has already, at the time the deposit is lodged, been the subject of a public announcement by the Post Office.)

Door-to-door distribution of unaddressed leaflets

The household delivery service   This service provides for the delivery of unaddressed material on a door-to-door basis in virtually any size of area required, whether it be a small town or village or the whole country.

No stamps are required and items may be enveloped or unenveloped provided they meet the following conditions:

Minimum size: 100 mm × 70 mm
Maximum size: 300 mm × 160 mm (larger items can be delivered by arrangement)
Normal maximum weight: 60 g
All items in a distribution are identical and bear the name and address of the sender.

Delivery will normally be completed within two weeks of an agreed starting date apart from December when the service is not generally available. Bulk supplies of items are, however, required one week in advance of the agreed starting date.

Prices vary according to the weight of the items involved and the total volume of the distribution. An additional charge is also made for the delivery of items which exceed the maximum dimensions. Full details can be obtained from your local Postal Sales Representative.

Reply services

Business reply service For reply cards and envelopes printed under licence with a reply-paid design. Fee per reply received by the licensee: ½p in addition to first- or second-class postage (no postage charge to the respondent). Licence fee per address: £20 per year. Irish Republic: no service.

Freepost A reply-paid service for use where pre-printed cards/envelopes are not possible. A special Freepost address may be quoted in press advertisements, TV and radio commercials, leaflets, etc. Fee per reply received by the licensee: ½p in addition to second-class postage (no postage charge to the respondent). Licence fee per address: £20 per year. Irish Republic and Isle of Man: no service.

Subject to certain conditions, holders of Business Reply and Freepost licences, who receive more than 50,000 Business Reply and/or Freepost items per year, may apply for a discount on the ½p additional postage fees paid. The scale of discounts is as follows:

Items received per year	Additional postage fees
50,000–99,999	½p per item less 40%
100,000–149,999	½p per item less 45%
150,000–299,999	½p per item less 50%
300,000–449,999	½p per item less 55%
450,000–599,999	½p per item less 60%
600,000–749,999	½p per item less 65%
750,000 and over	½p per item less 70%

Admail A contractual re-direction service for direct response advertisers who wish to quote an address local to the area of their advertisement's exposure, but have replies re-routed direct to their fulfilment house. This service is available within the UK postal area only. No service to the Irish Republic, the Isle of Man and the Channel Islands. Admail may be combined with the Freepost service, in which case normal Freepost charges will be made in addition to the Admail contract charge.

Compensation, registration and recorded delivery

Compensation The ordinary letter services are not designed as compensation services but compensation up to a maximum limit of £16.50 is payable where it can be shown that a letter was damaged or lost in the post due to the fault of the Post Office, its employees or agents. You are strongly urged in your own interests and in those of the addressee to obtain a Certificate of Posting and keep it in safe custody so that it will be available as evidence of posting if you should need to make a claim.

Compensation is limited to the market value of things lost or to the reduction in value of things damaged. It will not be paid for inadmissable articles (see the *Post Office Guide)* nor for damage to inadequately packed articles.

If you have special requirements or wish to send articles of higher value, the Post Office recommends the following special services obtainable for an additional fee.

Registration This service is particularly suitable for sending money and articles of higher value. It provides for evidence of posting, a signature on delivery and special handling arrangements throughout, but is not a safeguard against damage. Registered letters are sent by first-class post. For limits of compensation and current fees (in addition to postage), see the *Post Office Guide.*

Compensation will only be paid for money and certain monetary articles if a registered envelope sold by the Post Office is used. Under a new scheme, Consequential Loss Insurance, customers can protect themselves for a small fee against specific losses arising from a failure in the Inland registered post.

You may also send a registered packet in the cash-on-delivery service – see below under 'Parcels'.

Recorded delivery This service is designed for those who require evidence of posting and a signature on delivery. There is no special handling or security treatment and the service is more suitable for documents than the conveyance of articles of appreciable value. If the Post Office loses or damages a packet, compensation is payable up to a maximum limit of £18. There is no compensation for money, certain monetary articles, nor for jewellery sent by this service. (Again, see the Guide for details of the current fee.)

Advice of delivery This service is available for registered and recorded delivery items only. It may be requested at the time of posting, or afterwards (more expensive).

Parcels

There are two applicable rates for sending inland parcels – a national rate for parcels within the UK and to the Isle of Man, Channel Islands and Irish Republic; and an area rate which applies within a county or a specified group of counties. Cornwall and Devon, for example, is one area, so is Northern Ireland, and Middlesex. Unfortunately, area price concessions do not apply to London postal districts. (Full details of rates and areas are in the *Post Office Guide.)*

Special arrangements for businesses

The normal maximum parcel post weight is 10 kg. However, if you have a postage meter machine, you can post larger, heavier parcels (up to 22½ kg). For further details, contact your Postal Sales Representative. If you post more than 1,500 parcels per year, you may qualify for a parcel contract with the Royal Mail. Contract-holders can dispense with weighing parcels, sticking on stamps, or using postage meters. The Post Office can also arrange collection of the parcels from your business premises.

Cash-on-delivery service

This service is available within the UK and from the UK to the Channel Islands and the Isle of Man, but not to the Irish Republic. You can send the following items in the service with an invoice value of up to £300: ordinary parcels; compensation fee parcels; registered packets.

The Post Office collects payment and passes it on to the sender; invoice values over £50 are only collected on Post Office premises.

Postage forward parcel service

This service is designed to meet the needs of trading organisations who wish to obtain a parcel from a customer without putting him to the expense of paying the postage. The customer is sent an unstamped addressed label, wrapper or container with a special design. The design may be incorporated in newspaper advertisements or other publications for use as an address label. The parcel is posted in the ordinary way but without a stamp, and the addressee pays the charges on all such parcels he receives. The service does not operate to the Isle of Man, the Channel Islands or the Irish Republic.

Compensation

Although the ordinary inland parcel service is not designed as a compensation service, compensation up to a maximum limit of £16.50 is payable where it can be shown that a parcel was lost or damaged in the post due to the fault of the Post Office, its employees or agents. You are strongly urged in your own interests and in those of the addressee to obtain a Certificate of Posting and keep it in safe custody so that it will be available as evidence of posting if you should need to make a claim for compensation. If you wish to send articles of greater value the compensation fee parcel service should be used. Whichever service is used, compensation will be limited to the market value of the item lost, or to the reduction in value of items damaged. Compensation is not payable in certain circumstances – see the Post Office guide.

Compensation fee (CF) parcels

A parcel for an address in Great Britain, Northern Ireland, the Channel Islands, the Isle of Man or the Irish Republic may be sent as a CF parcel. You may also send a CF parcel by the cash-on-delivery service. Compensation is payable for a parcel lost or damaged in the post within certain limits according to the fee paid. There is no special handling or security treatment en route. No compensation can be paid for damage to inadequately packed articles. There is no compensation for money and certain monetary articles sent in CF parcels. Full details of this service are given in the Post Office Guide.

Newpapers and magazines

Newspapers and magazines distributed by post

Copies of publications including any supplements which have been registered as newspapers at the Post Office may be sent by the inland newspaper post and are given the same service as first-class letters. The publications must be specially posted by the publishers, printers or agents. All other newspapers are transmitted as first- or second-class letters according to the postage paid.

There is a small fee payable for registration as a newspaper. For details of this and newspaper and magazine postage rates, see the Guide.

Royal Mail special services

Datapost

Datapost provides a fast, secure, highly reliable overnight delivery service for urgent packages. It is available in two forms:

1 Scheduled datapost Packages are collected from customers at agreed times and delivered the next morning, also at agreed times. The service is available on a contractual basis for regular postings. Charges are negotiated individually taking into account weight, frequency of service and customer requirements. Discounts are available for regular and high-volume users.

2 On-demand datapost This service is designed for customers with less regular posting requirements. It offers the same reliability as the scheduled service and is available on either a contractual or non-contractual basis. Customers paying by account must use a nominated posting point. Customers who prefer to pay for their items at the time of posting can use any of nearly 1,600 main Post Offices throughout the UK. Payment can be made by cash, cheque (suitably backed) or meter frank.

Both the above services are available to a number of overseas countries. Applications for Datapost services should be made to your local Postal Sales Representative. If you require details, telephone 01-432 1919/1920.

Expresspost

Expresspost is a fast messenger collection and delivery service available in London using radio-controlled motor cycles and vans. It is also available in certain other large towns and cities. In addition to local services within the particular area, there are also many same-day inter-city links between Expresspost centres. Charges are based on distance.

Royal Mail special delivery

This service provides delivery by a Post Office messenger for letters and packets arriving at a delivery office on the next working day after posting but too late for normal delivery on that day.

In addition to first-class postage a Royal Mail special delivery fee of £1.50 must be paid. A certificate of posting will be issued. Items must be posted at Post Office counters in advance of latest recommended posting times for next working day delivery.

The special delivery fee will be refunded to the sender in respect of any item posted in advance of latest recommended posting times which does not receive delivery on the next working day after posting.

This service is not available to the Irish Republic, the Channel Islands and the Isle of Man.

Express delivery

To the Channel Islands, Isle of Man and Irish Republic. This service provides for delivery of a letter or packet by Post Office messenger after arrival at the office of delivery provided it arrives at a time when messengers are available and also provided that this will ensure earlier delivery than by normal postal treatment. Express delivery packets are sent from the office of posting to the office of delivery in ordinary mails.

Intelpost

Intelpost is a high-speed facsimile service, for the transmission of urgent copies between 60 Intelpost centres in the UK and to certain towns and cities in the USA, Canada, the Netherlands, Sweden and the Channel Islands.

Documents up to A4 size may be handed in at Post Offices

displaying 'Intelpost here', or can be collected by messenger on payment of an additional fee. At their destination, copies can either be picked up from the local Intelpost centre or delivery by messenger can be arranged.

Within this country transmission can also be made direct from customers' own compatible facsimile equipment to Intelpost centres for either counter pick-up or messenger delivery. This facility is available on account only. Customers may also hand over documents for transmission by Intelpost direct to recipients with compatible facsimile machines.

For full details of the service, please contact your local Postal Sales Representative or telephone Freefone 2463.

Electronic post

Electronic post is a new, computer-based service for bulk mailings. It can produce addressed and enveloped letters, statements, etc., from data supplied on computer tape by the customer. The service is on trial in two centres – London and Manchester – which between them can cover seven million addresses.

Outgoing mail services

The Post Office provides a number of collection services – some free and others at varying fees, depending upon whether the collection is made in town or in the country and on the number and frequency of letters or parcels collected.

In-coming mail services

Redirection

This service is invaluable if you are moving to a new business or private address. Redirection may be initially for a period of one, three or twelve months and may be prolonged for up to a further period of twelve months. The fees for redirection are relatively small in comparison to the inconvenience of having your mail go astray.

Delivery at another address (diversion)

For an annual fee, you can have mail which is addressed to your business address delivered to your private address or *vice versa*. Similarly, mail can be diverted from one branch of your business to another.

Retention of postal packets

If you do not want your mail to be delivered, the Post Office will retain it for a fee for a period of up to two months. There is no charge for retention up to five weekdays at Christmas and Easter, or up to three weekdays during the Spring or late Summer Bank Holidays.

This service is intended for business premises and is available for residential premises only in exceptional circumstances.

A variety of other incoming mail services may be provided on request or by special arrangement. These include private boxes and private bags, special search at the Post Office of delivery for a particular item and even 'Selectapost', whereby your mail will be subdivided before delivery, e.g. into the separate departments of your business.

Miscellaneous

Miscellaneous postal services include pre-stamped inland and overseas stationery, light-weight self-sealing packs with air-filled linings to protect the contents, strong card boxes for parcels and a variety of special supplies and services for the philatelist.

Overseas postal services

There are four main categories of overseas post and also International Datapost. Personal communications and taped messages may be sent only at the letter rate. Parcels to some countries may contain a letter for the addressee (see the Post Office Guide).

Letters

This is the simplest and speediest service for sending letters, postcards or goods up to 2 kg. Packets, which might be mistaken for other mail categories because of their appearance, should be clearly marked 'letter'.

Aerogrammes are a pre-paid light-weight letter sheet and combined envelope which are a comparatively cheap and convenient way of sending letters by air to countries outside Europe.

Printed papers and small packets

There are cheap rates for printed matter. The two categories of items are:

1 Commercial: advertising and publicity matter, catalogues, price lists, etc.
2 Literary: newspapers, books, periodicals, etc.

There is a single postage structure for printed papers sent by air mail with the exception of newspapers and periodicals on the Post Office Register, for which there is a special rate.

There is a similar special all-up rate for newspapers and periodicals to Europe. For other printed papers only a surface service is available.

There are two structures for printed papers sent by surface mail:

1 Full rate: for commercial items.
2 Reduced rate: for literary items.

In addition there is the small packet service for goods up to 1 kg (a few countries allow only 500 g).

Both printed papers and small packets must be packed so that they can be opened easily for examination, unless permission has been obtained from the Post Office for them to be sealed. Sealing permits are provided to regular large users of the service. Apply to your Head/District Postmaster.

The items must be clearly marked as appropriate, i.e. Printed Paper, Printed Paper Reduced Rate, Newspaper Rate, Newspaper All-up Rate or Small Packet. Letters or taped personal messages may not be included.

Postcards, Christmas, birthday and other greetings cards, change of address and visiting cards can be sent as printed papers at either surface full rate or air mail rate, provided they contain not more than five words of conventional greeting in addition to any printed text and a signature. The five words may be added by hand or by mechanical process. Cards in the above list which do not have the form, consistency and size of a postcard must be sent in unsealed envelopes when sent as printed papers.

Special printed paper contract services are available for bulk postings. Apply to the Postal Sales Representative at your local Head/District Post Office.

Swiftair

An express service for letters to Europe and for air mail letters and printed papers to countries outside Europe. It provides accelerated treatment in the UK and express delivery abroad where available.

Items must either be handed over a Post Office counter or included in a firm's collection. They should bear a Swiftair label and also air mail labels where appropriate.

The size and weight limits are the same as for ordinary letters and printed papers. Items can be registered or insured.

Parcels

Parcels may not exceed 1.05 m in length and 2 m in length and girth combined. The normal weight limit is 10 kg but in many cases it is possible for frequent users of the service to post parcels up to 20 kg. Air parcels and the associated despatch note (CP2) where required should bear blue Air Mail labels. Blocks of 4 labels should be used on the parcels.

International Datapost

Services for the conveyance of business and/or commercial papers and in some cases merchandise to a number of countries. For details of prices, standards of service and other information, contact your local Head Postmaster or telephone 01-432 1919/1920.

Customs and VAT requirements

All goods sent abroad by post, whether in letter packets, small packets or parcels, must be declared to Customs on special forms. These are available from Post Offices or as standard packs (for easy completion) from the following firms:

Moore Paragon (UK) Ltd,
75-79 Southwark Street,
London SE1 0HY.

Formecon Services Ltd,
Douglas House,
Gateway,
Crewe CW1 1YN.

Goods exported by post are exempt from VAT but each item valued at over £10 must bear the VAT label obtainable from Customs VAT offices. A Post Office Certificate of Posting is now sufficient proof of export for customs purposes (VAT forms 443, 445 and 446 are no longer necessary). All loose documents should be placed in an adhesive envelope and securely taped to the parcel. These envelopes are obtainable from post offices.

Please consult the *Post Office Guide* for full details of various services, e.g. eligibility of contents, methods of packing, size limits, dangerous substances, etc.

Thanks

Despite the complaints we all make, the British postal service is still, in general, magnificent. If in doubt, try your luck in most other countries. Businessmen need to know not only current postal rates (which, I repeat, change too often to be included in this appendix) but also how best to make use of postal services available. This appendix should be useful; supplement it by questions to the Post Office authorities concerned – and lavish a little time, thought and care on what is bound to be a very costly part of your business. A little consideration may produce a considerable saving in time as well as money.

Meanwhile, my thanks to the Post Office for their co-operation and help in preparing this guide.

Abbreviations and Foreign Usage

There is more than one form of shorthand (see Chapter 49). But the best way to shorten correspondence is often to use abbreviations. Sometimes these are charmingly English and even ancient Anglo-Saxon in origin. Sometimes they have crept in from foreign tongues – which, on occasion, provide expressions for which there is no useful English equivalent.

There now follows a list of abbreviations and foreign terms in common use. These are culled from vast numbers and if the initials which follow your name are not included, please do not be offended. Regard the list rather as a random sample for your use – and be glad that you will not need to look up initials which are your own.

a/c   Account
ack   Acknowledge
ad hoc   For this occasion
ad idem   As one, e.g. the minds of contract makers
a fortiori   Even more so; with added force
alter ego   A person's 'other self'
amicus curiae   A friend of the court; generally, counsel who appears
    out of courtesy to the court and not representing a client
am   *Anti meridiem*; before noon
ARIBA   Associate of the Royal Institute of British Architects
au fait   Fully conversant (or expert) in a matter

BA   Bachelor of Arts
BC   Before Christ
BCom   Bachelor of Commerce
BD   Bachelor of Divinity
BM   Bachelor of Medicine
BMA   British Medical Association
Bona fide   In good faith
BSc   Bachelor of Science
BSI   British Standards Institution
Bt or Bart   Baronet

Cantab   Of Cambridge University
CB   Commander of the Order of the Bath
CBE   Commander of the Order of the British Empire
CBI   Confederation of British Industry
c/f   Carried forward
cif   Cost insurance freight
C-in-C   Commander in Chief
CMG   Companion of Order of St Michael and St George
c/o   Care of
COD   Cash on Delivery
contra   Against
Cr   Credit or creditor

DBE   Dame of Order of British Empire
DD   Doctor of Divinity
DDS   Doctor of Dental Surgery
de facto   In fact (often, as opposed to *de jure*)
de jure   In law; as a matter of law
de novo   Again; anew
ditto   The same
Dr   Doctor; debit or debt

E&OE   Errors and ommissions excepted
e.g.   For example
ex   From or out of

FAI   Fellow of Auctioneers Institute
FIPM   Fellow of the Institute of Personnel Management
fob   Free on board
for   Free on rail
FRCP   Fellow of the Royal College of Physicians
FRCS   Fellow of the Royal College of Surgeons
FRIBA   Fellow of the Royal Institute of British Architects

GC   George Cross
GM   George Medal

HE   His Excellency or His Eminence
HM   Her Majesty (or Her Majesty's)
Hon   The Honourable
HRH   His Royal Highness (or Her Royal Highness)

i.e.   *Id est*; that is

inc.   Incorporated – Ltd in the USA

in flagrante   Caught in the act

IOU   I owe you

JP   Justice of the Peace

KB   Knight of the Bath or Knight Bachelor

KCB   Knight Commander of the Bath

KCMG   Knight Commander of the Order of St Michael and St
   George

mala fide   In bad faith

MD   Doctor of Medicine

modus operandi   A method of operation or plan of working

MP   Member of Parliament

MRSA   Member of the Royal Society of Arts

nem.con.   No one voting against

non seq.   *Non sequitur* – something that does not follow

o/d   Overdraft or overdrawn

OHMS   On Her Majesty's Service

Oxon.   Of Oxford University

PhD   Doctor of Philosophy

Plc   Public limited company

post meridiem   afternoon

post-mortem   After death

pp   *Per procurationem* or on behalf of

Pres.   President

prima facie   At the first glance

Prof.   Professor

ps   Postcript – that which comes after

pto   Please turn over

QC   Queen's Counsel

qed   *Quod erat demonstrandum* – which was to be proved, i.e. we
   have proved that which we set out to prove

qv   *Quod vide* – which see

RA   Royal Artillery; or Royal Academician
RAF   Royal Air Force
RSVP   *Respondez s'il vous plait* – please answer
rtd or rd   Refer to drawer
Rt Hon.   Right Honourable
Rt Rev.   Right Reverend

Seriatim   In a series
sine die   Without another date being fixed – indefinitely
sine qua non   Something without which you cannot manage, hence a
   necessity
status quo   Existing situation
SSP   Statutory sick pay
stet   It stands – normally, to restore words which have been crossed
   out. Or: leave as previously
sub judice   Under consideration by the court

TUC   Trades Union Congress

ultra vires   Beyond the powers (usually of a company or of a court)

vade-mecum   Something which should go with you always; a
   regular companion
verbatim   Word for word
Very Rev.   Very Reverend (as to Dean)
v.   *Vide* – see
videlicet   *viz.,* – namely
VP   Vice President

Style – and the Press

Letterwriters poke fun at 'journalese'. This is a mistake. Journalists are trained to use words accurately, precisely and with economy. Their papers often lay down 'rules of the house', specifying the style, punctuation or wordage to be used or abhorred. These are commonly contained in a 'Style Book'.

One of the best style books was put together by *Pulse,* a controlled circulation newspaper received by every general medical practitioner. By kind permission of its editor, here are some hints which commercial letterwriters would do well to note – although some are matters of taste, rather than rules of letter-writing law.

Style should at all times be aimed at achieving accuracy, clarity and readability. It should also be authoritative . . . remember that if you don't understand a phrase few readers will. Check and recheck and never take a chance and leave it in.

Adjectives, overuse of

Too many adjectives defeat their own purpose. Simplicity is the keynote of good style and any word this is not doing a job is superfluous. Watch for common tautologies such as 'broad daylight', 'completely untrue', 'definite decisions', 'cherished beliefs' – and for such descriptions as 'well known' (if the person referred to is well known, there is no point in saying so).

Spelling – US and GB

Many Americanisms have become absorbed into the English language . . . 'teenager', 'commuter', 'baby-sitter'. Others have not and should be avoided. It's also 'colour' not 'color' – except of course in 'Technicolor', but then that is a trade name.

Anglicised words

Many foreign words, too, have become accepted English usage and require no special treatment. But in the case of some French words the retention of the accent (acute) may sometimes be necessary.

Capitals

Avoid too many capitals. The fashion now is to knock them down except, of course, in abbreviations or where a specific reference is made – for example, 'Lower Biggleswade's Health Committee' but subsequently 'the committee' or 'health committee'. The Government is always capped if specifically the British; not, if not.

Collective nouns

These take a *singular* verb. Not 'The Health Committee/Government are' but 'The Health Committee/Government *is*'. Again there are obvious exceptions. You cannot, for example, say 'The police is' though you could say 'The police force is'.

Formal words

Avoid long-winded, pompous words where there are perfectly good one-syllable equivalents – for example, 'send' not 'despatch', 'about' not 'concerning', 'need' not 'necessity'.

Mixed metaphors

Unmix them. There was a good example recently: 'Those who slide down Moran's ladder will find it but a mere aperitif to the more grisly ladder of working conditions, status and salary that will inevitably await them.' (See also Chapter 18.)

Paragraphing

The look of the page is aided by good paragraphing. It adds horizontal to vertical space. Too little paragraphing gives a dull, shabby appearance, too much looks watery. For general guidance, no paragraph should run to more than fifty words.

Punctuation

Curb the tendency to over-punctuate. Punctuation is only an aid to sense. Too many commas and full stops merely confuse. Three short sentences are better than one which contains a number of subsidiary clauses. A colon always immediately precedes a direct quote. (See also Chapter 11.)

Quotes

Modern practice is for direct quotation to be carried in *single* quotes. Example – He said: 'Listen to me.' If the speaker is reporting what someone else has said, then it's *double* quotes inside single quotes. Example – He said: 'When I spoke to her, she said, "Listen to me!".' Which style you use is, of course, entirely a matter for you.

Hyphens

Words like today, midday, tomorrow, no one, are never hyphenated. ('No one' is *not* one word but two.)

Slang

Slang words are rarely acceptable but there are exceptions. Some words which were once slang are not slang now, others are on the borderline. It is a matter of common sense.

Index

Abbreviations:
  acceptability in business world,
    127
  form of shorthand, as, 123, 126
  list of those in common use, 231–4
Acceptance, as constituent of
  contract. See Contract
Acknowledgement:
  appreciation, of, 107
  form letters, use of, 12–15
  use of 'we', justification for, 47
Action, legal:
  burden of proof in, 205–6
  cost of, 203, 205
    taxing of, 205
  debt, for:
    going to trial, costs and
      disadvantages, 205
    jurisdiction, 204
    writ or summons, issue of, 204
  documents. See Documents
  evidence, types of, 206
  letter before:
    advantages of, 204
    cost of, 204
  negligence, for, matters to be
    proved, 178
  presentation of case in, 205–6
  procedure in courts, 208
  right of audience, 207
Address. See Envelope, style of
  address
Addresses, list of useful, 130–33
Adjectives:
  avoiding overuse of, 235
  use of, 30

Affidavit:
  declaration in lieu, 173
  discovery of documents to
    support, 209
  liability of deponent for contents
    of, 174
  meaning of, 173
  perjury in, 173
  summary judgement, to obtain,
    173–4
  swearing of, 174
Agent, authority, 174
  absence of, contract in, 190
  ostensible, 190
Allegations:
  persistent, strong rebuttal of,
    57–8, 68
  tactful replies to, 67, 73–4
Americanisms, use and avoidance,
  235
Annual Press Directory, 14
Apology:
  admission of liability, when
    construed as, 69
  precedents of, 70
Appeal. See Charitable appeals
Appreciation:
  acknowledgement of, 107
  customer or client, to, 107
  hospitality, of, 105
  offer, of, with tactful refusal, 107
  opening and closing, precedents
    for, 105–6
  services rendered, for, 108

Bank manager, letter to, 15

Baronet, style of address, 16–17
'Bread and butter' letters, opening
   and closing, precedents for,
   105–6
Brevity:
   advantages of, 28–9, 58, 82–3
   journalistic standards, 28
Business efficiency, interpretation
   of contract, 32
Burden of proof:
   civil action in, 206
   criminal proceedings, in, 205–6
   posting, of. *See* Posting

Carbon copy, use of, 121–2
Catalogue, postscript enclosing,
   14
Charitable appeals:
   brochures, points for and against,
     112
   covenant forms, use of, 112
   examples of, 110–11
   fund-raisers, rules for, 111–12
   personal note, enclosure with,
     110–11
   self-interest, playing on, 109
Church dignitaries, styles of address,
   17–18
Civic dignitaries, styles of address,
   18
Clarity, 31–3
Clichés:
   avoidance of, 33–4
   examples of, 34
   rudeness, as aid in replying to,
     74–5
Company, representation in court
   proceedings, 207
Complaints, effective use, 64
Condolences:
   formula for, 104
   on:
     death of husband, 103, 105
     death of wife, 103
   religion, offering comforts of, 104

Confidential mail, legal position,
   181–2
Congratulations on:
   achievement, 103
   honour conferred, 103
   promotion, 103
   recovery from illness, 103
Consideration, contract, in. *See*
   Contract
Contract, 187–91
   acceptance:
     conditional, counter-offer, as,
       188
     post, by, 213
     receipt of goods as, 188
     telex, by, 213
     unconditional, must be, 188,
       189
   agent, entering, 190
   conditions in small type, whether
     binding, 188
   consideration:
     absence of, effect, 189
     meaning of, 189
     necessity for, 189
   deposit, effect of, 190
   employee, by, when binding
     employer, 190
   employment, of. *See* Contract of
     employment
   essential elements of, 187–8, 191
   formalities of, 187
   infant, by, special requirements,
     189
   mental disorder of party, effect
     on, 189
   offer:
     invitation to treat distinguished,
       188
     unconditional, must be, 188
     what constitutes, 187–8
   oral, confirmation of in writing,
     advisability of, 187
   payment of deposit, rights created
     by, 190

terms, determining, 189
vagueness, when unenforceable
   for, 190–91
'without prejudice' letters,
   stemming from, 210
writing, whether necessary, 187
Contract of employment, 193–4
   importance of, 89
   notice provisions, 191
   repudiation by employee:
     summary dismissal, as grounds
      for, 195
     what amounts to, 195
   restraint clauses in, 191
   termination, methods of, 195
   variation, confirmation of, 193
   writing, whether necessary, 193
   written particulars:
     entitlement to, 193
     example of, 194
     matters to be contained, 193–4
     part-time employee, non-
      application to, 194
     set form, whether prescribed,
      194
     time within which to be
      supplied, 193
Copy correspondence, 10, 121–2
Copyright:
   collected correspondence, in, 113
   commissioned work, in, 167
   duration of, 166
   employment, arising from work
     done in course of, 167
   infringement, 167–8
     civil remedies, 167–8
     criminal sanctions, 168
     injunction to restain, 168
     measure of damages, 168
     photocopying machine, by, 168
     what constitutes, 167–8
   libraries, privilege of, 167
   meaning of, 166
   ownership, contrasted with, 165
   who owns, test as to, 166–7
   works in which subsisting, 166
Copyright Act 1956, 166
Correspondence:
   addressing. *See* Envelope, style of
     address
   copyright in, 113, 165
   famous persons, of, collections
     and valuation, 112–14
   menu card, etc., use for, 114
   public functions as opportunities
     for, 114–15
   style. *See* Style
   without prejudice. *See* Without
     prejudice
County Court:
   jurisdiction of, 204
   procedure in action in, 208
Courtesy title, style of address to
   holders of, 17
Courts, jurisdiction of, 204, 207
Customers and their customs, 76–9

Debtors, form letters to, 14–15
Declaration, affidavit in lieu of, 173
Defamation:
   action for:
     costs in, 171
     legal aid, in, 171
     matters to consider before
      commencing, 171
   references, and, 82, 169
   fair comment, extent of, 170
   justification, plea of, 169
   'knocking' goods of others, 172–3
   libel:
     avoidance of, 60
     meaning of, 169
     slander, distinguished from,
      169
   malice, 170, 173
   meaning of, 169
   privilege. *See* Privilege
   qualified privilege, 169
   slander:
     goods, 172

libel, distinguished from, 169
  meaning of, 169
  title, 172
Dictation, techniques of, 136, 140
Dictating machine:
  advantages of, 134
  battery operated, problems
    arising when, 137
  choice of, points to consider, 134
  guide to use of, 136–7
  indication of when tape has been
    used, 138
  microphone technique, 138
  servicing, 134
  size and type, choice of, 134
  spares for, 134
Dictionary, choice of, 30
Direct mail, meaning of, 127
Directories, use of, 129
Disclaimer:
  negligence, consequences avoided
    by, 82–3, 176–7
  reference, to accompany, 82–3
Dismissal:
  letter on, 54
  summary, meaning, 195
Disparagement. *See* Defamation
Doctor, style of address, 18
Documents:
  discovery:
    affidavit in support, 209
    identification, requirement of
      208
    inspection of, 209
    meaning of, 208
    pleadings, documents referred
      to in, 208
    privilege from, 209, 210
  importance in litigation, 206

Editor, letters to:
  covering note, advantages of, 100
  editorial policy:
    attacking, 99, 101
    supporting, 100

fair comment, what constitutes,
    97–8
  last word, editor always has, 99
  letter enclosing, 100, 101, 102
  opening and closing styles, 98, 102
  publication, rules to secure, 97
  rules for, 97–8
  telephone call prefacing, 98
  topicality, cogency of, 98
Electoral Register, use of, direct
    mailing, 129
Employee:
  contract by, when binding, 190
  error in letter typed and signed by,
    whether binding on
    employer, 180–81
  letters addressed to, right to open,
    181–2
  method of addressing, 16
  negligence of, liability of
    employer, 178–81
  notice, leaving without, rights of
    employer, 197
Employment:
  application for, 89–93
    curriculum vitae, use of, 92–3
    examples for adaptation, 89–93
    false modesty, avoidance, 91
    identification of prospective
      employer's interests, 93
    opening, 89
    rejection of, 95
    selectivity, necessity for, 92–3
  contract of. *See* Contract of
    employment
  copyright in work done in course
    of, 167
  interview for, 94–5
    expenses of attendance, law as
      to, 94
  invitation to, 94
  offer of appointment following,
    94–5
  offer of:
    following interview, 94–5

rejection of, 95
restraint, clause. *See* Restraint
  clause
retirement, after, application for,
  95–6
Enclosures:
  lists and schedules, 8–9
  reference at foot of letter to, 9, 11
Envelope:
  accuracy of address, 120
  direct mail, importance of, with,
    127
  personal attention, marking for,
    121
  quality of, 120
  typing on, attention to, 120

Filing
  referencing as aid to, 10
  system:
    importance of, 121-2
    individual needs, creation for,
      121
    intelligent use of, 122
    simplicity as keynote, 122
First person singular:
  public speaking, avoidance in, 48
  use of, 47–8
Flattery:
  apparent sincerity as keynote, 50
  examples for use and adaptation,
    49–54
  hiring and firing, use in, 51, 54
  praise as weapon of, examples,
    55
  sarcasm, danger of mistake for, 50
  subtlety, 50
  suspicion engendered by
    overdoing, 50
Follow-up letters, examples of, 80–81
Foreign usage, terms drawn from,
  list of, 231 *et seq*
Form letters:
  acknowledgements, use for, 12–14
  debtors, to, 15

Grammar, 24–7
  formal, when to ignore, 26–7
  means of improving, 25–6
  seal of education, as, 25

Handwriting, interpretation of, 75
Hedley Byrne v. *Heller and Partners*,
  176–7
HM Forces, officers of, style of
  address, 18
High Court:
  divisions, allocation of cases
    between, 207
  procedure in action in, 208
Humour, 36–40
  examples of application, 39–40
  'in' jokes, discretion in use of, 38
  irony, examples of gentle use,
    37–8
  limited scope for, 37
  pun, 36–7
  racial, dangers of, 79–80
  sarcasm:
    flattery mistaken for, 50
    occasions for, 37
  sting in the tail, 38–40
  surprise element developed by,
    39–40

Illness, congratulations on recovery
  from, 103
Infant, contract by, how far binding,
  189
Infringement of copyright. *See*
  Copyright
Injunction, reasons influencing
  court asked to grant, 196–7
Interpretation, 32
Introduction:
  disclaimer to accompany, 82–3
  examples of, 82–3
Invitation, tactful refusal, 107

Jargon, avoidance of, 77

Judgement debt, enforcement,
    methods of, 204

Knight, style of address, 16
'Knocking':
    malice as ingredient of, 173
    trade puffery, distinguished from,
    173
    when actionably defamatory, 173

Lady of title, style of address, 16–17
Landlord and Tenant Act 1954,
    notices under, 211–12
Layout:
    continuation sheets, use of, 11
    margins and spacing, 11
    specimen form of, 12
    standard style, 11
Legal action, *See* Action
Legal luminaries, style of address, 18
Letter:
    copies of, 10
    corrections to, 7
    dear, use of in, 4
    enclosures, use of, 8–9
    finish of, 4–6, 17, 23
    layout of, 10–12
    lists and schedules to, 8
    posting of, 217–22
    references on, 9, 12
    selling by, 87–9, 128
    shape of, 3
    standard form, 12–14
    start of, 4–6, 23
        direct mailing, 128
    style of, 23–4
    system for writing, 15
Letterheads, 119
Letter-writing, occasions for, 114–15
Libel. *See* Defamation
Library, privilege as to copyright,
    167
Lies, 70–75
    facts of business life, as, 72
    perjury. *See* Perjury

replies to, 73–5
rules for telling, 71–2
Lists:
    enclosures, as, 8
    inclusion in body of letter, 8–9
    names of, for direct mailing, 129
Litigation. *See* Action

Magistrates Court, 207
Mail:
    opening of, legal position, 181–2
    security, letters and parcel bombs,
        182
    selling by, 127–33
        addresses, useful, 133
        costing of, 129
        direct mail, meaning of, 127
        electoral register, use of, 129
        international lists of
            companies, 132
        international directories, 132
        letter, contents of, 128
        lists, keeping of, 128
        lists, names of, 129
        market research, 129
        reply card, use of, 128
        specialist directories, 129
        telephone and trade directories,
            use of, 129
        test mailing, 129
        useful addresses, 131–2
        useful publications, 130–31
Malicious falsehood:
    action for, 173
    malice, what constitutes, 173
Market research, 129
Mayor, style of address, 18
Member of Parliament, style of
    address, 18
Memory-jogger, examples for
    adaptation, 80–81
Merchantable quality, word
    processing and, 154
Metaphor, 41–2

mixed:
  avoidance of, 41–2, 236
  examples of, 41–2
Modern technology, 145–61
Modesty, 47–9
  editorial 'we', effect of, 47
  first person singular, use of, 47–8

Name:
  accuracy, importance of, 4
  Christian, familiar use of, 5, 16
  form at start of letter, 4, 15
  hostility, use to show, 4
  surname, 16
  See also Style of address
Negligence:
  action for, matters to be proved, 178
  damages for, 178–9
  disclaimer, when nullified by, 176–7
  duty of care, extent of, 177
    liability of employer, 178–81
  gratuitous information, whether applicable to, 176–7
  insurance cover against, 177
  reference, in giving, 177
Newspapers. *See* Editor, letters to
Non est factum, plea to obviate inference from signature of document, 175
Notes:
  memory, as jog to, 123
  objects of, 123
  personal. *See* Personal notes
  precision in taking, how to attain, 123
  preliminary to dictation, 122
  shorthand, advantages of, 123–5
Notice:
  employee leaving without giving, 196–8
    damages, measure of, 197–8
  provisions, 195

Oath, meaning of, 173–4
Offer:
  contract, as basis of. *See* Contract
  tactful refusal of, 107
Office system, importance of, 12–13
Officialese, 35–6
Overseas customers, 76–9
  choice of language when writing to, 77
  interpreter, danger of employing, 78

Parcels. *See* Postal services
Patent, threat of action for:
  infringement, remedies of person threatened, 172
Peerage, style of address, 17
Perjury:
  affidavit, in, 172
  meaning, 172
  penalties, 172
Personal notes, 75–6
  addenda to printed documents, as, 76
  advantages of, 75
  charitable appeal, enclosure with, 110–11
  menu cards, etc., use for, 123
  object of, 75–6
  public functions as opportunities for, 123
  'topping and tailing', typed letters, 75
Photocopiers, infringement of copyright by, 168
Post Office Guide, contents and purpose of, 217, 230
Postal services, 217–30
  advice on delivery, 222
  bulk posting:
    rebate, rate of, 218
    receipts, 218
    second-class mail, 217
  business reply service, 220
  certificate of posting, 221, 223

compensation, 221, 223
consequential loss insurance, 221
Datapost, 224
direct mailing deposit system, 219
discounts, 218
diversion, 226
door-to-door distribution,
    unaddressed leaflets, 219–20
electronic post, 226
express delivery, 225
express post, 225
first class mail, 217
    discount on, 218
household delivery service,
    219–20
incoming mail services, 226–7
Intelpost, 225
letters, 217–22
newspapers and magazines, 224
outgoing mail services, 226
overseas postal services, 227–30
    customs and VAT requirements,
        229–30
    international Datapost, 229
    letters, 227–8
    parcels, 229
    printed papers and small
        packets, 228
    Swiftair, 229
parcels
    business, special arrangements,
        222
    cash on delivery, 222
    compensation, 223
    postage forward service, 222–3
price protection, 219
recorded delivery, 221–2
redirection, 226
registration, 221
reply services, 220–21
    admail, 220
    business, 220
    discounts, 220
    freepost, 220
retention of postal packets, 227

Royal Mail special services, 224–6
second class mail:
    bulk posting, 217
    discounts, 218, 220
Selectapost, 227
special delivery, 225
Posting:
    acceptance of offer by, 212–13
    date on letter, evidential value,
        213
    post-book, value as evidence, 213
    proof of, direct evidence, by, 213
    time and date, postmark as
        evidence, 213
Postscript enclosing catalogue, 14
    standard, 14
    use of, 7
Praise as weapon of flattery,
    examples, 51–5
Precedent letters, 14, 23, 31
Press. *See* Editor, letters to
Price list, postscript enclosing, 14
Privilege:
    absolute, when attaching, 169
    discovery of documents, in,
        209–10
    qualified, 169–70
        malice destroys, 170
        reference, in giving, 169
Professional copywriters, use
    of, 128
Pro-forma letters, layout of, 14
Prosecution, burden of proof in,
    205–6
Punctuation, modern usage, 27

Quotes, modern practice in use of,
    237

Records, proof of actions taken, 63
Reference:
    disclaimer to accompany, 82–3
    examples of, 82–3
    letter, on, 9–12
    See also Referencing

negligence in giving, liability for, 176–7, 181
qualified privilege of giver, 169
Referencing:
  filing, as aid to, 9–10
  general, contents of, 10
  identification of writer and typist, 10
Reminder:
  appreciation coupled with, 108–9
  examples of, 80–81
Restraint clause, 32, 191–3
  examples of, 192–3
  prima facie contrary to public policy, 192
  reasonableness, test of, 192
  when enforceable, 32, 192
  whether severable, 193
Retirement, application for employment after, 95–6
Roget's Thesaurus, as guide to choice of words, 30
Rudeness, 56–62
  absence of superscription to signature as, 56
  carefully chosen, examples of, 57–9
  choice of words for, 57
  foul language distinguished, 57
  private and confidential correspondence, 60
  rebuttal of persistent allegations, 57–8
  riposte to, 58, 59, 60–62, 74–5
  rules for replying to, 61
  turning the other cheek, 65

Sarcasm:
  flattery mistaken for, 50
  occasions for use, 37, 58
Schedules as enclosures, 8
Secretary:
  contract of service, 139
  error in letter typed and signed by, whether binding on employer 180–81

making the best of, 139–40
methods of finding, 133
self-employed, advantages of, 133
signature of letters by, 7, 180–81
Secret information, use by exemployee, 191
Sedition, meaning of, 171–2
Self-expression, correspondence as form of, 26–7
Selling by letters, 87–9
  mail by, 127–133,
  See also Mail, selling by
Sentences, roles of, 26
Shorthand:
  abbreviations as form of, 126
  advantages of, 125–6
  methods of learning, 124, 126–7
  use by managers and executives, 123–4, 126
Signature:
  binding effect of, 174
  legal document, 175
  non est factum, pleas of, 175
  position of, 11
  secretary, by, 7
  style of, 6–7
  superscription, without, when intentionally offensive, 58
Sign-offs, use of 5, 7
Simile:
  advantages of use, 41
  examples of, 41
Slander. *See* Defamation
Slang, caution in use of, 237
Standard form letters, 12–15
  printing of, 14
  word processing, and, 145
Start of letter:
  commensurate style of ending, 4–6
  usage and etiquette, 4–6
Stationery:
  impression created by, 119–20
  professional designer, use of, 119
  shop window effect of, 119

Style, 23–4
    address, of. *See* Style of address
    adjectives, overuse of, 235
    Americanisms, use and avoidance,
        235
    anglicised foreign words, 235–6
    capitals, use of, 236
    collective nouns, verbs used with,
        236
    formal words, 236
    hyphens, care as to, 237
    impression created by, 23
    intention of letter, as reflection of,
        23
    layout, coincidence with, 23
    mixed metaphors, 236
    paragraphing, rules for, 236
    punctuation, minimising, 236–7
    quotes, recommended use of, 237
    slang, caution in use of, 237
    spelling, 235
Style of address, 15–19
    baronets, 16–17
    barristers, 16
    children of peers, 17
    Christian name, 16
    church dignitaries, 17–18
    civic dignitaries, 18
    doctors and surgeons, 18
    duke, 17
    earl, 17
    employees, 16
    female, 18
    knights, 16
    ladies, 16–17
    legal luminaries, 18
    marquess, 17
    mayors, 18
    Members of Parliament, 16–18
    more than one person, 18–19
    officers of HM Forces, 18
    peers, 17
    privy councillor, 18
    surname only, 15–16
    viscount, 17
    viscountess, 17
Sueing, letter before action, 58

Tact and tactics, generally, 45–83
Tact, use in disarming allegations,
    66–7
Telex, acceptance of offer by, 213
Testimonial:
    disclaimer to accompany, 82–3
    examples of, 82–3
'Thank you', opening and closing,
    precedents for,105–9, 108
    et seq.
    105–9
Trade directories, use of, 129
Translation, use of, 78
Typewriter:
    choice of, matters for
        consideration, 135
    electric, advantage of, 135

Unfair dismissal, 195–6
    compensation, 195
    considerations tribunal takes
        into account, 206
    legal aid, and, 196
    qualification for, protection, 195

Vicarious liability, 179–81

Warnings:
    examples of, 63–5
    power to implement, importance
        of, 64
Wit, use of, 34, 36–40
'Without prejudice', letters marked:
    binding agreement made by, 210
    court's ability to look at, 210
    protected, how far, 209–10
    unreasonable delay, 211
    waiver of privilege conferred, 212
Word processing, 145–61
    advantages, 146
    assessing requirements, 156–8
    automatic single-sheet feeder, 153

buying, leasing, renting, 156
checklist of facilities, 159–60
common uses, 145
computers and, 148
dealers, approaching, 158–9
desks, 155
distribution logic system, 150
environment for, 155
floppy disks, diagram, 151
industrial relations implications,
   160
legal protection, 154
lighting, 155
machines available, 146–7
maintenance and after sales,
   153–5
need for, 145
noise, 156
power supply, 155
printer, 152–3

problems, solving of, 160–61
remedies when breakdown, 154
repetitive work, use for, 145
reports, 146
running costs, 158
screen display, types of, 157
shared logic system, 147–9
shared resource system, 148
standard, 147
standard letters, 145–6
static electricity, 155
storage, 148–52
types of, 147–8
Words:
   choice of, guides to, 29–31
   clarity, examples of importance
     of, 31–2
   weapons, use as, 68
Wrongful dismissal, meaning, 195